STEP

U...

Lotus 1-2-3
on the
Amstrad PC

STEP BY STEP

Using
Lotus 1·2·3
on the
Amstrad PC

HEINEMANN
NEW·TECH

Heinemann Newtech
An imprint of Heinemann Professional Publishing Ltd
Halley Court, Jordan Hill, Oxford OX2 8EJ

OXFORD   LONDON   MELBOURNE   AUCKLAND   SINGAPORE
IBADAN   NAIROBI   GABORONE   KINGSTON

First published 1988
Reprinted 1989, 1990

British Library Cataloguing in Publication Data
Humpage, David G.
   Step by step guide to using Lotus 1-2-3
   1. IBM PC microcomputer systems.
   Spreadsheet packages: Lotus 123 – Manuals
   I. Title
   005'.369

ISBN 0 434 90802 9

Designed by JCA John Clark and Associates Ltd, Ringwood, Hampshire
Typeset by Colin Powell Typesetting, Bournemouth, Dorset
Printed and bound in Great Britain by
Biddles Ltd, Guildford and King's Lynn

Contents

Contents

Introduction: welcome to Lotus 1-2-3

Lotus 1-2-3 is probably the best selling spreadsheet package in the world, having outsold all other spreadsheet packages virtually since its introduction in 1983. Such popularity is testament to the power of 1-2-3, its flexibility and its speed of operation. Literally thousands of businesses and individuals rely on 1-2-3 to efficiently manage their data in a variety of ways and for a variety of reasons. Yet, despite its power, 1-2-3 is easy to use and within a very short period of time it is possible to have the spreadsheet up-and-running and producing useful information for you or your business. Once the fundamental principles have been mastered, quite sophisticated models can be built relatively quickly and easily.

As with all other spreadsheets, Lotus 1-2-3 is essentially a very large "sheet of paper" made up of small boxes or cells in which information can be placed for processing. The large capacity of 1-2-3 ensures that it can cope easily with even the largest models you may devise for it. The basic strength of spreadsheets is their ability to "number crunch" large amounts of data. Lotus 1-2-3 does this faster than probably any other spreadsheet currently on the market and, of course, with perfect accuracy.

But that's not all. Lotus 1-2-3 is an integrated package combining the power of its spreadsheet with Database Management, a Graphics Section and basic text editing. Consequently, the tasks which Lotus 1-2-3 can usefully perform for you are almost limitless, bounded only by your imagination to model a particular "problem" within the 1-2-3 parameters. Thus, from building a cash-flow forecast, preparing order forms and invoices, keeping track of customer and supplier records and managing an investment portfolio to producing a simple memo, can all be performed by Lotus 1-2-3 quickly and accurately.

Throughout this book all the above applications, and many more, will be explored and explained. The emphasis will be on *using* 1-2-3 and discovering its capabilities by seeing them in action. In a very short space of time you or your business will benefit from the investment you have made in Lotus 1-2-3.

I hope you find Lotus 1-2-3 as exciting to use as I have over the past few years and will marvel at its many capabilities. I'm sure you will enjoy using its many functions and will benefit from what it can do for you or your business with a little thought and application.

David Humpage

PART ONE

Before you begin

■ SECTION 1
Making your backup copies

Whatever software you buy, or files you create, you will be advised to make backup copies of your disks. This cannot be stressed too much. There is nothing worse than having spent good money on software, or valuable time on creating files, to lose them through some small error. Lotus 1-2-3 is no exception and working copies of the disks should be made as a priority. You should then use only the working copies, and store the originals in a safe place only to be retrieved should it become necessary to make a further working copy because your first one has become unusable. This may well seem unlikely, but if it should ever happen you will be very grateful for the fact that you took a little time to make a backup copy and can use the original to make a further copy.

The one difference with Lotus 1-2-3 is that the system (or program) disk is copy-protected by Lotus and hence cannot be copied. Consequently, in your 'package' of disks you will notice there are two system disks. One of these should be used as your working copy and the other stored in a safe place just in case the working copy should become corrupted. At the time of writing, Lotus has announced that all future copies of 1-2-3 will have the copy-protection removed so that backup copies can be made 'as normal'. You should check with your supplier before you purchase to establish whether or not the version you are buying is copy-protected or not.

Copying the disks

1   Cover the write-protect notches on the original disks. This is just a safety precaution to prevent any accidental over-writing of the original disks.

2   Boot up your PC with the MS-DOS operating system disk so that you have the A> prompt on screen. Leave the system disk in drive A.

3   Format four new disks on which to copy the Utility disk, Install Library disk, Printgraph disk and A View of 1-2-3 disk. This is achieved by typing:

   FORMAT B:

Making your backup copies

If you have twin drives, place your new disk in drive B and press Enter when you are ready.

If you have a single drive, press Enter and replace the system disk with your new disk when prompted to insert a disk in drive B.

4   Exit from FORMAT by typing N and pressing Enter when prompted by "Format another (Y/N)?", after your four new disks have been formatted.

5   Prepare the labels for your copies now. As you copy each disk affix the appropriate label so that you are certain to label each disk correctly.

6   Place the first original disk in drive A and type:

   COPY *.* B:

   and press Enter. If you have a twin-drive machine your newly formatted disk will be in drive B. If you have a single-drive machine you will need to swap disks when prompted to insert a disk in drive B.

7   Repeat the process for all four disks and store the originals, with one of the system disks, in a safe place and, except in an emergency, use only the working copies from now on.

8   In order to avoid being given a DOS error message every time you leave 1-2-3, it is necessary to copy the COMMAND.COM file from your operating system disk to the Lotus 1-2-3 system disk.

   To do this, place the MS DOS system disk in drive A and type, at the A> prompt:

   COPY COMMAND.COM B:

   If you have two drives, place the Lotus 1-2-3 system disk you intend to use as your working copy in drive B and press Enter.

   If you have one drive, press Enter and swap disks when prompted to insert disk in drive B.

   When COMMAND.COM has been copied to the 1-2-3 system disk, you will be returned to the DOS prompt.

■ SECTION 2
The Lotus Access system

In order that 1-2-3 can operate effectively with your equipment you must first tell 1-2-3 what equipment you have. This is achieved through the Install program.

You will require the following disks:

1-2-3 System Disk	A View of 1-2-3
Utility Disk	Printgraph Disk
Install Library Disk	

Each of the Lotus 1-2-3 companion programs can be started from the Access menus. To get this on screen, place the 1-2-3 system disk in drive A and, at the A> prompt,

> *Type* **LOTUS [Enter]**

After a few seconds you will see:

```
1-2-3  PrintGraph  Translate  Install  View  Exit
Enter 1-2-3 -- Lotus Worksheet/Graphics/Database program


                    1-2-3 Access System
                      Copyright 1986
                 Lotus Development Corporation
                    All Rights Reserved
                       Release 2.01

The Access System lets you choose 1-2-3, PrintGraph, the Translate
utility, the Install program, and A View of 1-2-3 from the menu at the
top of this screen.  If you're using a diskette system, the Access
System may prompt you to change disks.  Follow the instructions below
to start a program.

o  Use [RIGHT] or [LEFT] to move the menu pointer (the highlight bar at
   the top of the screen) to the program you want to use.

o  Press [RETURN] to start the program.

You can also start a program by typing the first letter of the menu
choice.  Press [HELP] for more information.
```

■ SECTION 2
The Lotus Access system

Read this information carefully. You will notice the Lotus Development Corporation copyright statement and information on the use of the Access System. In addition, you should find two lines at the top of the screen. The first of these lines is the MENU line showing the options:

```
 1-2-3    Printgraph    Install    View       Exit
```

The second line shows a description of the highlighted option or a submenu that will be displayed if that option is selected.

All Lotus 1-2-3 commands are accessed via such menus and each menu line follows the same format. To select a menu option you simply move the cursor with the left or right arrow key to highlight the function you require and press Enter. Alternatively, type the first letter of the option you require to select.

When the Access System is first loaded, the option **1-2-3** will be highlighted and the description line will read:

"Enter 1-2-3 . . Lotus Worksheet/Graphics/Database program".

Move the cursor once to the right to highlight **Printgraph**. Notice that the description line now changes to read:

"Enter Lotus Graphics Printing program"

Move the cursor to highlight the different menu options and check the descriptions of each one to familiarise yourself with what they will do.

■ SECTION 3
Installing your disks

When you have satisfied yourself as to what each item will do, we will install the disks using the **Install** program.

1   First, replace the 1-2-3 System disk in drive A with the Utility disk.

2   Move the cursor to highlight **Install** and the description line should read:

   "Start Install Procedure"

3   Press Enter to instruct 1-2-3 to begin the Install procedure.

It will take quite a few seconds for the Install program to load, but be patient and you will be rewarded with some general information about the install program as follows:

```
                    1-2-3 Install Program

                      Copyright 1985
                 Lotus Development Corporation
                    All Rights Reserved
                        Release 2


 The Install program lets you tell 1-2-3 what equipment you have.  You
 choose your equipment from a list of options by moving a highlight bar
 (the menu pointer) to your choice and pressing [RETURN].  You can start
 1-2-3 without using the Install program first, but you will not be able
 to see graphs or use a printer.

 If you need more information to make a particular choice, press [F1] to
 see a Help screen.  If you are a new user, make sure you have filled in
 the Hardware Chart in your 1-2-3 package before you begin.


 --------------- Press [RETURN] to begin the Install program. ------------
```

■ SECTION 3
Installing your disks

Read this information carefully before proceeding. Not only does it give specific information on installing your disks, but also general information about 1-2-3. In this case the general information informs you that if at any time you need more information about Lotus commands, you should press **F1** (function key 1).

On pressing Return or Enter, you will be asked first to insert the Install Library disk and then the Lotus 1-2-3 System disk, so have those to hand ready to proceed with Install. When finished, Lotus will display the **Install Main Menu:**

```
                        M A I N   M E N U
    _____


                                 _____

                                 : Select First-Time Installation:
    Use : or : to move menu pointer.    : for a guided path through the :
                                 : installation procedure.  This :
    First-Time Installation             : path lets you select drivers  :
    Change Selected Equipment           : for screen display and for    :
    Advanced Options                    : printers.
    Exit Install Program                :




                                 _____


    _____

    : and : move menu pointer.          [F1] displays a Help screen.
    [RETURN] selects highlighted choice.  [F9] takes you to main menu.
    [ESCAPE] takes you to previous screen. [F10] shows current selections.
```

You will require **First Time Installation**. Should you change any of your equipment in the future, for example buying a daisywheel printer, you can use the **Change Selected Equipment** option to tell 1-2-3 about those items you have just changed.

Move the cursor, if necessary, to highlight **First Time Installation** and press Enter.

You should now follow the instructions on screen. They are quite straightforward and relevant information is given for each requirement in the box on the right-hand side of the main menu. To speed up the process, the list of questions you will be asked is produced below:

Can your computer display graphs?
How many monitors have you?
Type of display card installed?
Do you have a text printer?
Brand of text printer?
Model of text printer?
Do you have another text printer?
Do you want to print graphs?
Brand of graphics printer?
Model of graphics printer?
Do you have another graphics printer?
Do you want to name your driver set?

Each item is selected in the same way by highlighting the appropriate response and pressing Enter.

Save the selections you have made when prompted for the 1-2-3 System disk, the Install Library disk, the Printgraph disk and A View of 1-2-3 disk. When the installation procedure is completed, you will be returned to the Access menu.

■ SECTION 4
Starting 1-2-3

We are now ready to look at the 1-2-3 worksheet.

You can load 1-2-3 from the A> prompt as follows:

> *Type* **1-2-3 [Enter]**

Since we have the Access system on screen, we will load 1-2-3 from there by moving the cursor to highlight **1-2-3** and pressing Enter. Almost immediately the Lotus 1-2-3 logo and copyright information will appear on screen and after a few seconds you should see the following:

```
A1:                                                    READY

          A     B     C     D     E     F     G     H
   1
   2
   3
   4
   5
   6
   7
   8
   9
  10
  11
  12
  13
  14
  15
  16
  17
  18
  19
  20

  20-Nov-87   19:55 PM
```

■ SECTION 4
Starting 1-2-3

What you have on screen is just a small part of the 1-2-3 worksheet – the first eight **columns**, labelled A to H, and the first twenty **rows** labelled 1 to 20. In fact, Lotus 1-2-3 has a total of 256 columns, labelled A to IV (that is A to Z, then AA to AZ, BA to BZ and so on until IA to IV) and 8192 rows.

The labelling of the column letters and row numbers serve to identify **cells**, the smallest part of the worksheet in which you can enter and store data. The co-ordinates of a cell are always given column letter first followed by the row number. So, for example, the top left-hand cell is called **A1** and it should be currently highlighted by the **spreadsheet cursor**. You will notice that the cursor fills the whole cell. If you check back to the number of rows and columns supported by 1-2-3, you could soon calculate that a massive two million cells plus can be used for storing data.

We will see in Part 2 how to move around the whole worksheet and enter data into the cells, but first let us look at some other important information contained within this opening (blank) worksheet.

Starting from the top of the screen you should locate three lines which make up the **control panel**. The first of these lines should contain two entries. In the top left-hand corner is **A1:** which is the **current cell address**, i.e. the cell currently occupied by the cursor, and the contents of that cell. At the moment, this shows that A1 is blank.

The top right-hand corner should contain the word **READY**. This is the 1-2-3 **mode indicator** which currently indicates that 1-2-3 is ready to accept input from the keyboard. As we go through the various functions of 1-2-3 the mode indicator will change to reflect what it is you are doing.

The second line of the control panel is currently blank, but will display the current cell contents *as you type them* or a **menu** when you issue a command.

The third line is also blank, but will contain the **description** or **submenu**, just like the set-up of the Access system you saw a little earlier.

At the bottom left-hand corner of the screen you will see the **date and time indicator** which will display the date and time that you entered when starting DOS (or as supplied by the internal clock of your computer).

The bottom right-hand corner of the screen indicates various functions such as the Num Lock switched on, and these will be brought to your attention as they occur.

The important thing is that no matter what you are doing within Lotus 1-2-3, the screen will always give you an indication of what is going on. You should make full use of this information, particularly when you are developing the basic skills of spreadsheet manipulation.

■ SECTION 5
Some commonly used keys

Before we actually enter data into the worksheet it is worth making sure you can find your way around the 1-2-3 keyboard. Most of the keys operate as normal but you should locate, and note the responses of, both the function keys and some other important keys.

The function keys

Your function key template, which should be placed over the appropriate keys for your keyboard, gives relevant details of what each key will do. You may need to use the following function keys in the first few sections of the book:

F1 The **Help** key — which will display information about the 1-2-3 commands and operations.

F2 The **Edit** key — for amending cell entries.

F5 The **Goto** key — to move quickly to a particular cell address.

F6 The **Window** key — which allows you to toggle between the windows created.

Some commonly used keys

Other important keys

Forward slash   This is located towards the bottom right-hand corner of the keyboard beneath the question mark (?). You will use this key frequently since it provides access to the Lotus 1-2-3 command structure via the menus.

Esc or **Escape**   This is located towards the top right-hand side of the keyboard. Pressing the escape key within 1-2-3 will move you back through the menus one step at a time.

←Del or **Backspace**   This is located towards the top right-hand side of the keyboard close to the numeric key pad. This key will delete characters *to the left of the cursor* when in edit mode.

Del or **Delete**   This is located on the bottom right of the numeric key pad. This key will delete characters *at the cursor* when in edit mode.

Home   This is located at the top left of the numeric key pad (No. 7). Pressing the Home key will always take you to cell A1 from anywhere in the worksheet.

Arrow keys or **Cursor keys**   These are the numbers 2, 4, 6 and 8 on the numeric key pad (or they may be in a cluster of their own if you have an extended keyboard). These keys move the cursor about the worksheet in the direction shown by the arrow. They will also place the cursor in the required position when editing.

Enter   This key may be labelled with a right-angled arrow, the word Enter or the word Return. The Enter key is used to instruct 1-2-3 to carry out a command or to store an entry in a cell. If you have two keys on your keyboard with any of the above labels, then pressing either will have the same effect. (*Note:* throughout this book, in the lines instructing you to type something, [**Enter**] means 'Press the Enter key'.)

■ SECTION 6
If you make a mistake

Lotus 1-2-3 offers several ways to correct mistakes (I use most of them frequently), the best method being determined by the stage you are at when you discover the mistake.

■ If you make a mistake whilst typing and have not yet pressed Enter or moved to another cell, delete all the characters with the backspace key until the mistake has been erased and retype the remainder of the entry correctly.

■ If you have pressed Enter or moved to another cell, position the cursor in the cell containing the mistake, retype the entry and press Enter or move the cursor to another cell.

■ If you have a particularly long cell entry which would be tedious to retype, place the cursor in the cell containing the entry, press F2 (the Edit key) and use the cursor and delete keys in the control panel to amend the entry. Press Enter when the entry is correct.

■ When you start to build larger worksheets, you may find it necessary to erase whole sections of your worksheet. You should use the **/Range,Erase** command which is explained in Section 11.

■ The procedure to erase the whole of the worksheet is the **/Worksheet,Erase** command which is explained in Section 16.

PART TWO

A trip around the worksheet

■ SECTION 7
Moving around the worksheet

As you will recall, what you can see on screen is only a small part of the 1-2-3 worksheet and that there are over two million cells in which we could store data. It is therefore essential that we can move around the worksheet as quickly and easily as possible.

The most frequently used method will be to use the arrow or cursor keys as you move from cell to cell storing data. However, as you build larger and larger worksheets, it will become very tedious moving over large areas by just using the cursor keys. Let's try out some of the alternatives.

The Goto key (F5)

Press F5. Note that the Mode indicator has changed to POINT and you are prompted for an address to go to. This can be any address within the confines of the worksheet boundaries.

   Type **AA546** [Enter]

Almost instantaneously the cursor will be placed in the cell you have specified. Note that the current cell indicator on the control panel shows **AA546:** and that the cell is blank.

The Home key (No. 7 on the numeric key pad)

You can return to cell A1 from anywhere in the worksheet by simply pressing the Home key. Do this now and check that the current cell indicator shows **A1:**.

The End key

You will find this key very useful, particularly when building large worksheets or when using the database facility. It operates in conjunction with the cursor keys as follows:

1   Press the **End** key. Note this is indicated in the bottom right-hand corner of the screen.

2   Press the **down** cursor key.

What has happened? The cursor has moved very rapidly to cell location A8192, the very last row of the 1-2-3 worksheet. Try pressing the down cursor key once again and the computer will beep at you. That's as far as you can go. What the End key does is move the cursor in the direction of the cursor key used in conjunction with it, through a continuous range of cells. Since all the cells in our worksheet are currently blank, we can use the End key to visit the four extreme corners of the worksheet. Here goes!

■ Press End and then the → cursor key – the current cell indicator shows IV8192, the bottom right-hand most corner of the worksheet.

■ Press End and then the ↑ cursor key – you should now be in cell IV1.

■ Press End and then the ← cursor key – you are back in cell A1.

Big right

To move one screenful to the *right*, hold down the **Control** key and press the → cursor key. You should be in cell I1.

Pressing the **Tab key** has the same effect.

Big left

To move one screenful to the *left*, hold down the **Control** key and press the ← cursor key. You should be back in cell A1.

Holding down the **Shift** key and pressing the **Tab** key has the same effect.

PgDn (page down)

To move down the worksheet one screenful at a time, press the **PgDn** key (No. 3 on the numeric key pad). The cursor should be in cell A21.

PgUp (page up)

To move up the worksheet one screenful at a time, press the **PgUp** key (No. 9 on the numeric key pad). You should be back in cell A1.

Practice moving around the worksheet with each of the above keys until you become familiar with their operation. When you are building a worksheet, think about the cursor movement required and use the quickest method to get to where you want to go. A little thought beforehand can save you a lot of time!

■ SECTION 8
Changing the start-up directory

In the near future we will want to save the worksheet to disk. If you have a single disk drive you can skip this section and go straight to Section 10.

If you have two drives, you need to tell 1-2-3 to save all files to drive B. Here's how it's done.

Press the forward slash key (/). On screen you should have:

```
┌──────────────────────────────────────────────────────────────┐
│ A1:                                                   MENU     │
│ Worksheet Range Copy Move File Print Graph Data System Quit    │
│ Global, Insert, Delete, Column, Erase, Titles, Window, Status, Page │
│           A      B      C      D      E      F      G      H   │
│  1                                                             │
│  2                                                             │
│                                                                │
└──────────────────────────────────────────────────────────────┘
```

This is the beginning of the 1-2-3 Menu or Command structure. It operates in exactly the same way as the Access system, i.e. either highlight the option you wish to select and press Enter, or type the first letter of the option.

Note that the mode indicator has changed to **MENU** and the option **Worksheet** is highlighted.

We need to move to the **Default** option on the **Global** menu, so:

> Type **W** to select **Worksheet**
> Type **G** to select **Global**

If you move the cursor to the right to highlight **Default**, you will see:

```
┌──────────────────────────────────────────────────────────────┐
│ A1:                                                   MENU     │
│ Format  Label-Prefix Column-Width Recalculation Protection Default Zero │
│ Define default disk and printer settings                       │
│           A      B      C      D      E      F      G      H   │
│  1                                                             │
│  2                                                             │
│                                                                │
└──────────────────────────────────────────────────────────────┘
```

■ SECTION 8
Changing the start-up directory

Press Enter and you will see the following options:

```
: A1:                                                          MENU :
: Printer  Directory  Status  Update  Other  Quit                  :
: Specify printer interface and default settings                   :
:         A       B       C       D       E       F       G       H :
: 1                                                               . :
: 2                                                                 :
:                                                                   :
```

Type **D** to select **Directory**

You will be prompted for the **Directory** at start-up:

```
: A1:                                                          EDIT :
: Directory at startup: a:\                                         :
:                                                                   :
:         A       B       C       D       E       F       G       H :
: 1                                                                 :
: 2                                                                 :
:                                                                   :
```

Note that the mode indicator has changed to **EDIT**, indicating that
1-2-3 is prepared for you to amend the current entry. Press **Esc**, and
a:\ will disappear.
  Type **b:**

The control panel should now look like this:

```
: A1:                                                          EDIT :
: Directory at startup: b:\                                         :
:                                                                   :
:         A       B       C       D       E       F       G       H :
: 1                                                                 :
: 2                                                                 :
:                                                                   :
```

■ SECTION 8
Changing the start-up directory

Press Enter and you will be returned to the menu with Directory highlighted.

We now need to save this information on the 1-2-3 System disk. Remove the write-protect tab from the 1-2-3 System disk and place the disk back in drive A:

Type **U** to select **Update**

You will be prompted to place any blank, formatted disk in drive B. Then press any key.

Type **Q** to select **Quit**

and you will be returned to the worksheet in READY mode.

Whenever you instruct 1-2-3 to **Save** or **Retrieve** a file, it will now automatically search drive B.

Planning and design

The worksheet we are going to create is quite simple in concept. Consider a company that sells several products, the sales of which are affected by seasonal factors. For example, the products could be items of clothing, some of which sell well in the summer months and others which do better in winter. We want to create a model to show the sales on a quarterly basis, the total for the year and each quarter, the profit derived from the sales and the percentage revenue each product contributes to the total. The completed model could look like this:

```
A1: [W13] 'Quarterly Sales by Product - 1987                    READY

          A        B        C        D        E        F        G
                                                              % Of
  1  Quarterly Sales by Product - 1987
  2
  3                                                            Year   Total
  4                                                            Total  Revenu
  5                  Q1       Q2       Q3       Q4
  6  ------------------------------------------------------------------
  7  Product 1     2000     2250      900     3500     8650    19.70
  8  Product 2     2250     3500     3500     1250    10500    23.92
  9  Product 3      750     1000     1500     1000     4250     9.68
 10  Product 4     4000     3000     1000     3750    11750    26.77
 11  Product 5     1000     1500     2750     3500     8750    19.93
 12  ------------------------------------------------------------------
 13  TOTAL REVENUE 10000    11250     9650    13000    43900
 14  ==================================================================
 15
 16  Total Cost    6000     6750     5790     7800    26340
 17
 18  PROFIT        4000     4500     3860     5200    17560
 19                                                   =========
 20
```

■ SECTION 9
Planning and design

It will take us a little while to get to this stage, so *don't worry if your worksheet does not look like this when you first enter the data*. We will be making several amendments as we go along, particularly in Part 3.

Before launching into 1-2-3 to create the worksheet, it is worth considering the factors that culminated in the model above.

With any application, it is good practice to plan and design the worksheet before you begin. Even though it is relatively easy to change the worksheet, spending a little time beforehand with pencil and paper will reap dividends in the future. Not only will it save you time and frustration by getting it right first time, but you will also ensure that your finished model gives you the information you require.

As with the worksheet we are going to create, many sets of numbers are best shown in the form of a table. This makes the data easier to read and understand. Also, with an organised worksheet, you will find it easy to add to or amend the data to take account of any changes or additions required.

The model also follows convention in that the time element of the data (quarters in this case) runs horizontally across the worksheet, though it would have been just as easy to arrange the products horizontally and the quarters vertically. You will find this convention important when we come to creating graphs and charts in Part 4, but if you think about the data for this exercise you will find it to be the most sensible layout anyway. Whilst the company may add or delete products from its range, which can be easily incorporated in the model as it stands, the number of quarters in a year never changes. Consequently, even if several products are added to the range, the whole of the worksheet will be on the screen which you will find is easy to read. (We will look at the problems with larger worksheets that cover more than the screen in future sections).

Whilst not obvious at the moment, in the above worksheet much of the *work* will be done by 1-2-3. This arises through the use of formulae to calculate, for example, totals and percentages. This makes good sense since, generally speaking, 1-2-3 can calculate more accurately and quicker than you or I. You will also find it useful when you come to build larger worksheets, as shown in Section 26. So, use formulae whenever it is appropriate to do so.

■ SECTION 9
Planning and design

When planning the worksheet, the important things to remember are:

■ Consider each set of data individually and organise your worksheet to best accommodate the information you have.

■ Think about the information you want to get out of the worksheet – 1-2-3 can provide you with much useful information, but you need to organise your worksheet so that what you require can be achieved quickly and easily.

■ Organise the rows and columns in the light of both the above. The worksheet can be changed but you will find it saves you time if you get the basic design right at the start.

■ Most data is not static and can change over time. Make 1-2-3 work for you by using formulae where possible and appropriate. Should it be necessary, you will find making changes or amendments can be implemented quickly with the minimum amount of typing from the keyboard if appropriate formulae have been incorporated in the model.

■ SECTION 10
Making cell entries

Before we begin, a recap of what to do if you make a mistake:

■ If you have not pressed Enter or moved to another cell, use the backspace to delete characters to the left of the cursor until all the mistakes have been cleared, and retype the remaining characters correctly.

■ If you have pressed Enter or moved to another cell, place the cursor in the cell containing the mistake and retype the full entry. Alternatively, press F2, the Edit key, and use the cursor keys and delete keys to amend the entry.

Let's begin.

First, all worksheets should have a title. Place the cursor in A1 if it is not already there:

Type **Quarterly Sales by Product − 1987**

Before you press Enter notice what has happened to the 1-2-3 indicators. The Mode indicator now shows **LABEL**, indicating that 1-2-3 will treat the entry as a string of text. Also, the second line of the control panel shows exactly what you have typed. Check that your title is correct and amend if necessary.

To store the title in cell A1,

Either press Enter
Or move the cursor to new cell with the cursor keys

You should now enter the row and column labels in the cells as shown on the illustration of the completed worksheet. This will avoid any problems in entering the correct formulae in the next section.

Making cell entries

When you have entered all the labels, enter the quarterly sales figures as follows:

Cell	Data	Cell	Data	Cell	Data	Cell	Data
B7	- 2000	C7	- 2250	D7	- 900	E7	- 3500
B8	- 2250	C8	- 3500	D8	- 3500	E8	- 1250
B9	- 750	C9	- 1000	D9	- 1500	E9	- 1000
B10	- 4000	C10	- 3000	D10	- 1000	E10	- 3750
B11	- 1000	C11	- 1500	D11	- 2750	E11	- 3500

There are two things you should notice as you enter the above figures. First, as soon as you type the first number of each entry, the mode indicator changes to **VALUE** indicating that 1-2-3 will treat the entry you are making as a number.

Secondly, the numbers are aligned to the right of the cell in contrast to labels, which are aligned to the left by default.

At this stage, *do not* attempt to align the labels with the numbers neatly in each column. In particular, *do not* attempt to align numbers by typing spaces before the number since the entry will then be treated as a label. We will return to the problem of aligning labels within the columns or rows in Part 3.

You can now enter the Total cost figures as follows:

```
Q1 - 6000 in cell B16
Q2 - 6750 in cell C16
Q3 - 5790 in cell D16
Q4 - 7800 in cell E16
```

When you have entered the Total cost figure for Q1, the entry in cell A16, Total cost, will appear to have been truncated to 'Total cos'. What has happened is due to the fact that the default width of 1-2-3 columns is nine characters. Whilst there is no entry in the cell to the right, 1-2-3 will display the full entry, but once you put something in

Making cell entries

that cell then the other entry is restricted to the default nine characters. However, the full label is still stored by 1-2-3 and you can check this by moving the cursor to A16 and looking at the control panel. The current cell entry should still indicate 'Total cost'. We will see in Part 3 how to adjust the columns so that the whole label can be seen again, so do not worry about it just now.

If all has gone well and you have entered both labels and values, your worksheet so far should look like this (note it is assumed that your cursor is in cell A1):

```
: A1: 'Quarterly Sales by Product - 1987                    READY :
:
:
:         A        B        C        D        E      F        G      H :
: 1   Quarterly Sales by Product - 1987                               :
: 2                                                                    :
: 3                                                   % Of             :
: 4                                            Year   Total            :
: 5          Q1       Q2       Q3       Q4     Total  Revenue          :
: 6                                                                    :
: 7   Product 1    2000     2250      900     3500                     :
: 8   Product 2    2250     3500     3500     1250                     :
: 9   Product 3     750     1000     1500     1000                     :
: 10  Product 4    4000     3000     1000     3750                     :
: 11  Product 5    1000     1500     2750     3500                     :
: 12                                                                   :
: 13  TOTAL REVENUE                                                    :
: 14                                                                   :
: 15                                                                   :
: 16  Total Cos    6000     6750     5790     7800                     :
: 17                                                                   :
: 18  PROFIT                                                           :
:                                                                      :
```

We now need to instruct 1-2-3 to make various calculations for us and this is covered in the next section.

■ SECTION 11
Using simple formulae effectively

One of the beauties of the 1-2-3 spreadsheet is the ease and speed with which it performs calculations for you. For this particular model we only need three basic types of formulae: addition, subtraction and percentages. However, it may be useful just to say a few general things about formulae before we begin.

■   Formulae that include cell addresses operate on the contents of the cells you have identified, e.g. $+B6+C8$ means add the **contents** of B6 to the contents of C8.

■   In 1-2-3, operations are performed by calculating multiplication (*) and division (/) before addition (+) and subtraction (−). Consequently, $10+6-8/4$ will return an answer of 14, i.e.

    $8/4 = 2$
    $10+6 = 16$
    $16-2 = 14$

■   You can override precedence by putting parentheses around an operation since operations in parentheses, or brackets, are performed first and within the parentheses normal mathematical procedures apply. For example, $(10+6-8)/4$ will return an answer of 2, i.e.

    $10+6-8 = 8$
    $8/4 = 2$

■   When dealing with long formulae, as above, it is worth checking the result manually to ensure the formula you have written gives the answer you require. Generally, you should keep formulae to manageable proportions − it is so easy to get yourself lost if you are not careful.

■   A formula must be entered in the cell *where you want the answer to appear*.

■ SECTION 11
Using simple formulae effectively

So, in order to find the total yearly sales for Product 1, we must add together the contents of cells B7, C7, D7 and E7. With 1-2-3, this can be done in one of two ways:

Either type   **+ B7 + C7 + D7 + E7** [**Enter**]

Note that you *must* include the first plus sign to tell 1-2-3 that the entry is to be treated as a value and not a label.

Or type   **@SUM(B7..E7)** [**Enter**]

The formula must be typed exactly as shown and simply says add together the contents of the cells in the range B7 to E7. You should note that either one or two full-stops can be typed between B7 and E7, but 1-2-3 will always show two full-stops.

Alternatively, you could name the range to be summed (see Section 12), then

Type   **@SUM(range name)** [**Enter**]

All the methods will yield exactly the same result, so it doesn't really matter which one you use. Personally, I use the first method if there are only two or three cells to be added together and the second for all other additions since it is usually quicker. The third method would be used if you frequently needed to refer to the range you have named. Instead of typing or highlighting the range of cells, you could simply type the name.

Place the cursor in cell F7 (the cell where you want the answer to appear):

Type   **@SUM(B7..E7)** [**Enter**]

The answer, **8650**, should appear as if by magic. Note that even though the result of the formula is shown on your screen, the cell contents retain the formula itself.

Leave the yearly totals for now and we will see in the next section a way of speeding up the process of entering formulae in the relevant cells for the other products.

Move the cursor to cell B13 and we will enter a similar formula to sum the Quarterly totals:

Type   **@SUM(B7..B11)** [**Enter**]

The answer should be 10000?

Using simple formulae effectively

Now for the Profit. Profit is simply the total revenue received by the firm less the total costs, so the formula required in cell B18 is:

+ B13 – B16

Remember the plus sign before the cell address to instruct 1-2-3 to treat the entry as a value and not a label. The answer, 4000, should appear in cell B18.

We now need the last formula to calculate the percentage of the total revenue for each of the products. There are several ways of arriving at this formula, depending on how you like to deal with percentages. The easiest is probably:

+ F7/F13*100

This translates as, the contents of F7 divided by the contents of F13 and multiplied by 100.

When you enter this formula and press Enter, you will probably have a minor heart attack because what should appear in cell G7 is the message **ERR**. Don't worry, it is simply 1-2-3 telling you that it cannot perform the calculation we have requested because we do not have a figure in cell F13, i.e. we are asking 1-2-3 to divide F7 by zero. Once we enter the relevant formula to produce a figure in F13, which we will do in the next section, G7 will contain the correct percentage of the total revenue.

Using simple formulae effectively

If all has gone well your worksheet should look like this:

```
: A1: 'Quarterly Sales by Product - 1987                        READY :
:
:
:           A         B        C        D        E       F        G      H :
: 1     Quarterly Sales by Product - 1987                                  :
: 2                                                                        :
: 3                                                              % Of      :
: 4                                                      Year    Total     :
: 5            Q1        Q2       Q3       Q4    Total   Revenue           :
: 6                                                                        :
: 7     Product 1     2000     2250      900     3500    8650 ERR          :
: 8     Product 2     2250     3500     3500     1250                      :
: 9     Product 3      750     1000     1500     1000                      :
: 10    Product 4     4000     3000     1000     3750                      :
: 11    Product 5     1000     1500     2750     3500                      :
: 12                                                                       :
: 13    TOTAL REV   10000                                                  :
: 14                                                                       :
: 15                                                                       :
: 16    Total Cos    6000     6750     5790     7800                       :
: 17                                                                       :
: 18    PROFIT       4000                                                  :
: 19                                                                       :
: 20                                                                       :
:                                                                          :
```

If you notice any differences between what you have on screen and what is shown above, check the cell contents and make the necessary amendments before proceeding.

To complete the entries, we now need to enter the remainder of the formulae by copying those we have already entered, into the appropriate cells. This is the topic of the next section.

■ SECTION 12
Copying the contents of cells

To make life a little easier, 1-2-3 allows you to copy the contents of any one cell or range of cells to any other cell or range of cells. This is particularly useful in large spreadsheets but can also save you a great deal of time in a modest worksheet like ours. First a note on **ranges**.

■ In 1-2-3 (and other spreadsheets) a range is any rectangular block of cells and can be a single cell, a row, a column or several rows and columns. For example:

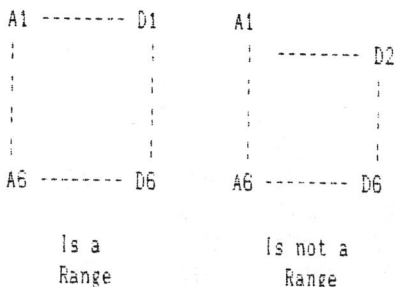

```
A1 -------- D1      A1
 :          :        :  -------- D2
 :          :        :           :
 :          :        :           :
 :          :        :           :
A6 -------- D6      A6 -------- D6

    Is a                 Is not a
    Range                Range
```

■ The range is identified by the addresses of any two diagonally opposite corners of the range, separated by one or two full-stops (or periods). In the above example, the range would normally be entered as A1..D6 but it could be entered as D1..A6. A single cell would be entered by the single cell address.

■ In 1-2-3, ranges can be entered in three ways:

1   Type the cell addresses.
2   Highlight the range by moving the cursor with the cursor keys.
3   Use a range name created with the **/Range Name Create** command.

Let's see it in operation within our worksheet.

First, place the cursor in cell F7 which should contain the formula @SUM(B7..E7). We are going to copy this formula (the contents of the cell) to cells F8, F9, F10 and F11.

Type   / to access the command menus
Type   **C** to select **Copy**

■ SECTION 12
Copying the contents of cells

You will be prompted for the *range to copy from* and F7..F7 will be offered as the range. Note that the Mode indicator has changed to POINT – more of this a little later.

We only want to copy the contents of cell F7, so simply press Enter. You will be prompted for the *range to copy to* and F7 will again be offered. At this stage, you can do one of two things: *either*

>   *Type*   **F8..F11** [**Enter**]

or

>   **POINT** to the range required
>   Move the cursor to cell F8
>   Press the full-stop key
>   Move the cursor to cell F11, noting that the range you are going to copy to is highlighted
>   Press Enter

Both methods will yield exactly the same result. If you check the contents of cells F8 to F11 you will find they are, respectively:

>   **@SUM(B8..E8)**
>   **@SUM(B9..E9)**
>   **@SUM(B10..E10)**
>   **@SUM(B11..E11)**

Notice what has happened. The formulae have automatically adjusted to their new position *relative* to the rows containing the cells to be added. This is known as **relative addressing** and is the default addressing used by 1-2-3. We will see another form of addressing a little later.

We also need to copy the same formula to cells F13 and F16 to give Total Revenue and Total Cost, respectively.

Place the cursor in any of the cells F7 to F11:

>   *Type*   /C to select **Copy**
>   *Type*   [**Enter**] to select the current cell as the cell to copy **From**.
>   *Type*   **F13** [**Enter**].

You should be able to repeat the process to copy the formula to cell G16.

You should also be able to copy the formula in cell B13 to cells C13, D13 and E13.

Copying the contents of cells

We now need to look at the formula in cell G7, the one for the percentage of total revenue. With this formula we require one of the values to remain the same no matter where in the worksheet we copy it to. This is the contents of cell F13 which contains the Total Revenue for the year of all products.

To achieve this we need to amend the formula slightly. Place the cursor in cell G7 and press F2 (the Edit function key). The contents of the cell appear in the control panel, second line.

Move the cursor so that it is under the F of F13,

   Type **$**

Move the cursor so that it is under the 1 of 13,

   Type **$ |Enter|**

Your formula should look like this:

F7/$F$13*100

If you now copy this formula to cells G8, G9, G10 and G11 and review their contents you will find they are as follows:

  F8/$F$13*100
  F9/$F$13*100
  F10/$F$13*100
  F11/$F$13*100

In other words, the formula always takes the yearly total in the *different* rows as a percentage of the total contained in cell F13. This is known as **absolute addressing**.

One can also combine relative and absolute addressing to give **mixed addressing**. This would appear as follows:

■   **$F13** — would always give the same column (F) but the row would change depending upon where the formula was copied to.

■   **F$13** — would always give the same row (13) but the column would change depending upon where the formula was copied to.

The concept of cell addressing is vital when copying formulae and you are advised to re-read the above to make sure you understand what will happen to formulae when you copy them using the different methods above.

■ SECTION 12
Copying the contents of cells

If you finally copy the contents of cell B18 to C18, D18, E18 and F18, your worksheet should now be complete and look like this:

```
: A1: 'Quarterly Sales by Product - 1987                      READY :
:
:
:           A      B        C        D       E      F       G        :
: 1   Quarterly Sales by Product - 1987                              :
: 2                                                                  :
: 3                                                  % Of            :
: 4                                          Year    Total           :
: 5          Q1       Q2       Q3      Q4    Total   Revenue         :
: 6                                                                  :
: 7   Product 1   2000     2250      900    3500     8650  19.70387  :
: 8   Product 2   2250     3500     3500    1250    10500  23.91799  :
: 9   Product 3    750     1000     1500    1000     4250   9.681093 :
: 10  Product 4   4000     3000     1000    3750    11750  26.76537  :
: 11  Product 5   1000     1500     2750    3500     8750  19.93166  :
: 12                                                                 :
: 13  TOTAL REV  10000    11250     9650   13000    43900            :
: 14                                                                 :
: 15                                                                 :
: 16  Total Cos   6000     6750     5790    7800    26340            :
: 17                                                                 :
: 18  PROFIT      4000     4500     3860    5200    17560            :
: 19                                                                 :
: 20                                                                 :
:                                                                    :
```

However, you will notice it does not look like the illustration of the completed worksheet shown at the beginning of Section 9. We need to improve the general appearance of the worksheet and this will be done in the next section.

PART THREE

Improving the appearance of your worksheet

Changing the format

Lotus 1-2-3 offers a wide range of functions to improve the appearance of your worksheet. These can either be used on the whole worksheet – **Global settings** – or on ranges of cells – **Range settings**.

The Global settings are accessed as follows:

Type / to access the command menus
Type **W** to select **Worksheet**
Type **G** to select **Global**
Type **F** to select **Format**

The formats available will be shown as:

```
: A1:                                                              MENU :
: Fixed  Scientific  Currency  ,  General  +/-  Percent  Date  Text  Hidden:
: Fixed number of decimal places (x.xx)                                :
:          A      B      C      D      E      F      G      H :
: 1                                                                    :
: 2                                                                    :
```

The same formats are available for a range of data and are accessed as follows:

Type /
Type **R** to select **Range**
Type **F** to select **Format**

We will use most of the formats available in 1-2-3 throughout the course of this book, but here is a brief description of what each will do. Once we have saved the worksheet you might like to experiment with the different formats to familiarise yourself with their effect.

Fixed format will allow you to set the number of decimal places displayed on screen. The default setting is for two decimal places but you can select any number from 0 to 15 inclusive.

Scientific format will display numbers in an exponential format, e.g. $1.24E + 2$, which means that the scientific format has been specified to have two decimal places and the number is 124.

■ SECTION 13
Changing the format

Currency format   Lotus is an American company and consequently the default currency format is American and takes the form of $x,xxx.xx. However, the $ sign can be changed to a £ sign from the Global,Default menu. Select **Other**, then **International**, and make the necessary change.

Comma (,) format   A comma is inserted to indicate thousands and also shows negative numbers in parentheses.

+ / − format produces a horizontal bar chart format.

Percent format multiplies the value by 100 and adds a percentage sign (%).

Date format allows you to change the way the date is displayed.

Text format will display formulae on screen rather than the resultant value.

Hidden format suppresses the display of cell contents.

The format we require for our worksheet is fixed decimal places so that we can avoid the awkward numbers in the percentage column.

Place the cursor in cell G7 using the cursor keys or the F5 Goto key. Then

> *Type*   /
> *Type*   **R** to select **Range**
> *Type*   .F to select **Format**
> *Type*   **F** to select **Fixed**
> *Type*   [**Enter**] to select the default setting of 2

You will then be prompted to enter the range and G7..G7 will be offered. You can then either type, for example, G7..G11, or highlight the range, and press Enter. The percentage figures will change to a more realistic two-decimal-places number.

You should note that the current cell content indicator now shows [F2] before the formula indicating that the cell has been formatted to two decimal places.

Alternatively, you could use the percent format, but you must amend the formula to take account of the multiplication by 100. The formula will now need to read + **F7/$F$13**. In addition, [P2] will be added to the current cell content indicator to remind you that the cells are formatted to Percent with **2** decimal places.

The % of Total Revenue column would look like this:

```
% Of
Total
Revenue

19.70%
23.92%
 9.68%
26.77%
19.93%
```

■ SECTION 14
Adjusting the column width

With long row or column labels we have seen that the contents are truncated when an entry is made in an adjacent cell. When you first enter 1-2-3 the column widths are set to nine characters by default. However, it is possible with 1-2-3 to have column widths from one to two hundred and forty characters inclusive.

A gentle warning however. Generally, whatever you produce with 1-2-3 will at some time be printed and so you must take account of the limitations of your printer and the width of paper it can handle.

If you want to set all the columns to a particular width (though you will usually find that it is individual columns that need to be adjusted), this can be done with the Global setting. You should proceed as follows:

Type   /
Type   **W** to select **Worksheet**
Type   **G** to select **Global**
Type   **C** to select **Column-Width**

You will be prompted for the global width, the current setting (9) being shown.

Now, there are two ways to set the column width, though both will yield exactly the same result:

1   Type the number of characters wide you want the column(s) to be and press Enter.

2   Use the cursor keys to expand or contract the column to the desired width and press Enter. The advantage of this method, particularly when adjusting a single column only, is that you can see the effect on the whole worksheet as well as the column itself, before you make the selection.

Experiment by typing any number between 0 and 240 or moving the cursor with the cursor keys and press Enter to see the effect. You will be surprised at the difference the column widths can have on the overall appearance of the worksheet. In particular, it can make the information easier to read — an important point when the finished product is printed out.

To return to the original settings, simply repeat the process and type 9 when prompted for the global width.

■ SECTION 14
Adjusting the column width

With our worksheet, not all the columns need to be reset since it is only column A that is causing a problem. So let's expand it a little so that we can once again see our full labels.

Move the cursor to any cell in column A:

Type **/**
Type **W**
Type **C** to select **Column**
Type **S** to select **Set-width**
Type **13** (or move the cursor to a width of thirteen) [**Enter**]

Column A will expand so that all your row labels are visible once again.

■ SECTION 15
Inserting/deleting rows and columns

Blank rows and columns can be inserted or existing rows and columns deleted anywhere in the worksheet. The **Delete** command should be used with a certain amount of caution, since once you have pressed Enter the row or column is lost forever and if you have made a mistake you will have to retype the whole of the data again. However, you will be pleased to know that all your formulae, including those with absolute addressing, will be automatically amended to take account of their new position in the worksheet.

When inserting rows or columns you should remember:

■　**Columns** are inserted to the *left* of the cursor.
■　**Rows** are inserted *above* the cursor.

I have always found it safer to have the cursor in the correct row or column *before* executing the command.

Let's experiment for a moment with the worksheet you have on screen by inserting a column between our row labels and the sales details for Quarter 1. First, place the cursor in any cell in **column B**:

Type　/
Type　**W**
Type　**I** to select **Insert**
Type　**C** to select **Column** [Enter]

The worksheet should 'part' to make space for the blank column we have just inserted.

Inserting/deleting rows and columns

```
| B1:                                                    READY |
|                                                              |
|                                                              |
|          A        B        C      D      E      F      G     |
| 1  Quarterly Sales by Product - 1987                         |
| 2                                                            |
| 3                                                            |
| 4                                                     Year   |
| 5                         Q1     Q2     Q3     Q4     Total  |
| 6                                                            |
| 7  Product 1            2000   2250    900   3500    8650    |
| 8  Product 2            2250   3500   3500   1250   10500    |
| 9  Product 3             750   1000   1500   1000    4250    |
| 10 Product 4            4000   3000   1000   3750   11750    |
| 11 Product 5            1000   1500   2750   3500    8750    |
| 12                                                           |
| 13 TOTAL REVENUE       10000  11250   9650  13000   43900    |
| 14                                                           |
| 15                                                           |
| 16 Total Cost           6000   6750   5790   7800   26340    |
| 17                                                           |
| 18 PROFIT               4000   4500   3860   5200   17560    |
| 19                                                           |
| 20                                                           |
```

Note that the column of data headed '% Of Total Revenue' has now disappeared off the screen. It has been forced to scroll to the 'next screen' so that the new blank column can be accommodated. You could, of course, enter data in this column in the normal way, but for the present let's just look at what has happened to the existing data now that it has been moved to a new location.

First, adding a new column has had no visual effect on *any* of the information we have entered. The labels and all the numbers, including the totals and percentages, have remained exactly the same.

Now move the cursor to one of the cells that contains a formula. Notice how the formula has been automatically adjusted to take account of the new cell locations. This happens no matter what type of formula you have entered, whether it be relative, absolute or mixed addressing. Altering the appearance of your worksheet could not be simpler since 1-2-3 will look after all your information for you to make sure the worksheet still produces the results you intended. However, it is always worth checking your formulae since there are times when 1-2-3 will not make the necessary adjustments for you.

Take a look at the rest of the formulae and satisfy yourself that each has been adjusted to compensate for the insertion of the blank column.

Try inserting a row in the worksheet, remembering that the row will be placed immediately above the cursor. Don't worry about the overall appearance of the worksheet — we will shortly delete the rows and columns you have just inserted. You can check the formulae again to see that they have been adjusted to take account of their new locations.

If you want to insert more than one row or column, before you press Enter move the cursor to highlight the number you wish to insert. If we had wanted to insert two columns previously, you would have simply moved the cursor once to the right before pressing Enter.

Your worksheet probably looks a bit of a mess now so let's delete the rows and columns you have just inserted and return to the original structure. A little more care is needed when using the Delete command since once the data has been deleted it is lost forever.

You should remember that rows and columns are deleted *at* the cursor. Again, I have found it best to have the cursor in the row or column to be deleted *before* executing the command.

Move the cursor to any cell in a blank column you have inserted:

Type /
Type W
Type D to select **Delete**
Type C to select **Column [Enter]**

The blank column should disappear and the other columns adjust to take its place. Follow the same procedure to delete any other blank columns you have inserted.

Deleting rows involves a similar operation. First, place the cursor in any cell of a blank row you have created. Then:

Type /
Type **W**
Type **D**
Type **R** to select **Row** [**Enter**]

The blank row should now disappear.

Delete all the blank rows you created until you are back to what you started with at the beginning of the Section. If you care to check, all your formulae should have been returned to exactly how you entered them in the first place.

Can I just repeat the warning given earlier about the care needed when using the Delete command. You will be most annoyed at yourself (and anybody else in close proximity) if you inadvertently delete a whole row or column of data you have just painstakingly entered and find you have to type the whole of it again. A little thought and a double check before you press Enter will save you a certain amount of frustration at the keyboard.

■ SECTION 16
Aligning and repeating labels

Whilst it is not possible to align numbers in 1-2-3, it is possible to align the labels. Thus, in particular, we can align the column headings so that they appear directly above the figures we have entered. You will find, especially when the worksheet is printed, that the information becomes much easier to read and understand.

Again, we can align all labels on the Global setting or individual and ranges of labels depending on the effect we want to achieve. They can be aligned to the left, right or centre of the cell in which they have been entered.

Note Labels can only be aligned as they are being entered (by including a label prefix in the entry) or after they have been entered. You can not 'pre-format' a blank cell to determine the alignment of a label that has yet to be entered.

Move the cursor to A1 by pressing the Home key and note exactly what is shown by the current cell indicator. It should show:

A1: 'Quarterly Sales by Product − 1987

Notice the apostrophe before the word Quarterly. You did not type the apostrophe, it was automatically added by 1-2-3 and indicates that the label is aligned to the *left* of the cell − the default setting. We can *force* 1-2-3 to align labels differently by typing a different label prefix. The three available in 1-2-3 are:

' − aligns labels to the *left* of the cell

^ − aligns labels in the *centre* of the cell

'' − aligns labels to the *right* of the cell

You may need to search the keyboard a little to find these symbols, though generally the apostrophe (') is just to the left of the Enter key and has a @ above it; ^ is typed by holding down the shift key whilst pressing the number 6 at the top of the keyboard (not the numeric key pad); the double quote (") is usually shift and number 2 at the top of the keyboard.

So, to align a label to the right *as you type it*, simply start the text with the quotation mark, type the label as normal and press Enter. However, I have always found it more economical to leave the alignment of labels until I have completed the worksheet. Only then can you get an overall picture of the data and determine the alignments that are necessary. If you align the labels as you type

Aligning and repeating labels

them, you may find that you have to alter them again when you have finished making all the entries.

If you wish to align all your labels to one particular setting then you need to use a Global command:

Type /
Type **W**
Type **G** to select **Global**
Type **L** to select **Label-prefix**

You should then have this menu on screen:

```
A1:                                                        MENU
Left  Right  Center
Align labels with left edges of cells
          A          B          C          D          E          F          G
1
2
```

Simply select the required alignment by pressing L, R or C (apologies for the spelling of *centre*, but as noted previously Lotus is an American company) or highlighting the selection and pressing Enter.

In many cases you will want to align a range of labels rather than every label in the worksheet. This is true of our worksheet. We want to keep the row labels aligned to the left, but the column labels need to be adjusted individually.

First, we will deal with the headings Q1, Q2, Q3, Q4 and Total Revenue. Place the cursor in cell B5, then:

Type /
Type **R** to select **Range**
Type **L** to select **Label**
Type **R** to select **Right**

You will be prompted to enter the range to be justified and the mode indicator will show POINT.

Move the cursor four cells to the right and then one row up so that all the labels to be aligned are highlighted and press Enter.

■ SECTION 16
Aligning and repeating labels

Notice that the current cell indicator on the control panel now shows the quotation mark prefix before the heading Q1 and that all the labels you highlighted are now aligned to the right of the cell.

The heading for column G requires the labels in G3 and G4 aligned in the centre and the word Revenue aligned to the right.

Move the cursor to G3:

Type   /
Type   **R**
Type   **L**
Type   **C** to select **Center**

then move the cursor down one cell to highlight the labels '% Of' and 'Total', and press Enter. The two labels should now appear in the centre of their respective cells.

Finally, the label in G5. You can either repeat the above process with the cursor in cell G5 and just press Enter when prompted for the range to align or you can press the Edit key (F2) and type in the quotation mark in place of the apostrophe.

Have a look at what you now have on screen compared to the illustration shown in Section 9. Yours should now look very similar except for the underlining of the labels and totals. This is the last amendment we have to make and involves another time-saving feature of 1-2-3 by which labels can be automatically repeated to fill a whole cell.

Place the cursor in B6:

Type   \ – [**Enter**]

(*Note*   In this line, \ is the **backslash** key which you will probably find just to the right of the shift key on the left-hand side of your keyboard. If the menus appear on the top of your screen, you will know that you have pressed the forward-slash key rather than the backslash key. Simply press Escape to exit the menus and then press the backslash key. The ' – ' is the minus sign, or hyphen, key.)

The whole cell should now be filled with minus signs which are generally used for underline purposes in 1-2-3. Whatever character is typed after the backslash will be repeated throughout the whole cell. So, for example, if you wanted to underline a heading or other piece of text with asterisks (*) you could simply type * and the whole cell would be filled with asterisks by 1-2-3.

■ SECTION 16
Aligning and repeating labels

The whole cell will always be filled, no matter how wide the cell is and the contents will automatically adjust if you should alter the width of the cell at a later date.

Having filled B6 with minus signs you should now copy its contents to cells C6..G6 in the same way we have copied cell contents previously. You can also repeat the process for row 12 which separates the totals from the individual items of data.

For the double underline immediately below the totals we need to use the equals sign (=). First place the cursor in B14, then:

Type \ = |**Enter**|

You can now copy the contents of B14 to the remaining cells in row 14 until all the totals are double underlined.

Finally, if you check back to the illustration in Section 9, you will find that the final profit for the year was also double underlined.

Place the cursor in F19 then:

Type \ = |**Enter**|

Your worksheet is now complete and should match exactly the illustration we started out with in Section 9. Having got this far, you can give yourself a pat on the back for you have successfully used many of the basic commands within 1-2-3.

Having produced this worksheet we will save it to disk, print out a copy on your printer and clear the screen ready for a new worksheet.

■ SECTION 17
Saving and retrieving your worksheet

One of the major advantages of any computer application is that the information can be stored to disk and recalled at any time.

Organising your files on disk is an important operation and using appropriate file names can save you a lot of time in the future should you want to recall a particular worksheet. Any file name should indicate the contents of that file so that in a month or two it offers a reminder of what is stored in it.

It is recommended that you store your spreadsheet files on a separate disk from the 1-2-3 system disk. This is for two reasons:

■ It will prevent any accidental corruption of the programs on your system disk.

■ It will give you more space in which store your files.

If possible, 1-2-3 files should also be stored on disks which do not contain other types of file, e.g. word-processing or database files.

As your System disk should have a write-protect label adhered to it, it will also save you the hassle of having to remove it every time you want to save a file.

If you have twin drives on your computer, and have followed the directions for specifying the start-up directory, 1-2-3 will automatically save your files to the disk in drive B. If you have a single drive, you will need to remove the system disk from drive A and replace it with the formatted disk on which you intend to store your spreadsheet files.

To save the worksheet you have just created, first press the Home key to take the cursor to cell A1. This just ensures that the cursor will be in A1 when you retrieve the file at a later date:

Type   /
Type   **F** to select **File**
Type   **S** to select **Save**

■ SECTION 17
Saving and retrieving your worksheet

You will be prompted for a file name:

```
  A1:                                                          EDIT
  Enter save file name: B:\

         A        B       C       D       E       F       G       H
  1
  2
```

Note that the 'data' drive specified is drive B since we set the directory in Section 10.

If you had retrieved a file and were now in the process of re-saving it, the menu above would show the name of the file you had retrieved. You can then simply press Enter to save the file with the same name and *replace* the existing file on disk. Since we have created a brand new file, we need to type in a file name.

First a note as to the way 1-2-3 stores the data you create. A three-character **extension** is automatically added to the name you give to a file. There are three possible extensions:

.WK1 Used for all worksheet files. In addition to the actual data you have entered in the worksheet, 1-2-3 also stores all the formats, column widths, etc., you have used to create the worksheet. Consequently, when you retrieve the file it is exactly the same as when you saved it.

.PIC As we shall see later, this file extension is used on all graph files you wish to be printed. This includes not only the graph or chart itself, but also the titles, keys and axis labels.

.PRN Used for all print files. This allows you to print the file directly from disk rather than first loading it into the worksheet area, e.g. from DOS or a wordprocessor.

So let's type in a file name and see that the file has been correctly saved with the appropriate file extension. Type any file name (but no longer than eight characters), or may I suggest

   Type   **QSALES [Enter]**

Saving and retrieving your worksheet

The light on the disk drive will illuminate, the disk will revolve and you will be returned to the ready mode when the file has been saved.

Let's just check that the file has been saved:

Type /
Type **F** to select **File**
Type **L** to select **List**

You will be prompted to select from:

```
/------------------------------------\
:  Worksheet  Print  Graph  Other  :
\------------------------------------/
```

You now have the following options:

Type **W** – displays all Worksheet files stored on your disk
Type **P** – displays all Print files
Type **G** – displays all Graph files
Type **O** – displays all the files on your disk

You shouldn't have many files on your disk at the moment but we will ask 1-2-3 to display all that you have:

Type **O** to select **Other**

Your worksheet screen should be replaced by:

```
:                                                                    :
: A1:                                                          FILES :
: Name of files to list: B:\*.*                                      :
:          QSALES.WK1    10/19/87      20:23         7620            :
: QSALES.WK1                                                         :
:                                                                    :
:                                                                    :
:                                                                    :
:                                                                    :
:                                                                    :
:                                                                    :
:                                                                    :
:                                                                    :
:                                                                    :
:                                                                    :
:                                                                    :
:                                                                    :
```

Saving and retrieving your worksheet

Some useful information is shown on this screen even though as yet we only have one file stored on the disk. First you will notice that the .WK1 extension has been added by 1-2-3 to the file you have just saved. Also notice that some general information is given about the file that is currently highlighted:

■ *The name of the file* is repeated – QSALES.WK1. File names will always be shown in upper case (capitals) by 1-2-3.

■ *The date the file was saved.* In my case it was 19 October 1987; in your case it will be the current date or the date you entered on starting DOS.

■ *The time the file was saved.* In my case it was 20.23, in your case it will be the current time.

■ *The size of the file in bytes.* This is 7620 and yours should be something very similar.

To return to your worksheet and the ready mode press Enter.

Passwords

To prevent anyone other than yourself from being able to retrieve a file, 1-2-3 offers the facility of storing the file with a password. Only on entering the correct password can the file be retrieved. **If you forget the password, there is no way to retrieve the file.** Consequently, you should think very carefully about the password you use. You need a word that you are not going to forget, yet is not obvious to anyone who is 'illegally' trying to retrieve the file. (The names of children and pets are just two of the obvious ones that 'hackers' try first.)

To save the filename with a password, follow the same procedure as for saving a file normally. When you have entered the file name, press the spacebar then:

   Type   **P** [**Enter**]

You will be prompted to enter the password:

   Type   **'Password'** [**Enter**]

Note that a small box is displayed rather than the characters you have typed. You will be prompted to **Verify** the password by typing it in again.

■ SECTION 17
Saving and retrieving your worksheet

If you make a mistake whilst typing the password the second time, 1-2-3 will beep, the mode indicator will flash ERROR and you will be informed in the bottom left-hand corner of your screen that the passwords do not match. You will then need to press Escape to return to READY mode and repeat the whole sequence (or consider that perhaps you do not really need password protection).

To change or delete the password you must first retrieve the file and then follow the procedure as if you were going to save it again. The name of your file will be followed by [**Password protected**].

If you wish to use the same password, press Enter. If you wish to change the password, press Esc or Backspace, then the spacebar, then:

Type   **P** [**Enter**]
Type   **'New password'**

To delete the password, press Esc or the Backspace key and then press Enter.

Having saved the worksheet to disk, you can now clear the screen. You could then begin a new worksheet, load another file into the worksheet area or, what we will do for the next section, retrieve the same file ready for printing.

To clear the screen:

Type   **/**
Type   **W**
Type   **E** to select **Erase**

You will be prompted to type **N** if you do not want to erase the worksheet and wish to return to READY mode and **Y** if you are sure you want to erase the worksheet. If you select Yes, you should now have on screen a blank worksheet. When you retrieve a file, you will find that the process is quicker if you load into a blank worksheet rather than replacing an existing worksheet.

We will retrieve the worksheet you have just saved to disk so that we can prepare to print it:

Type   **/**
Type   **F** to select **File**
Type   **R** to select **Retrieve**

■ SECTION 17
Saving and retrieving your worksheet

You should see the following on screen:

```
A1:                                                          FILES
Name of file to retrieve: B:\*.wk?
QSALES.WK1
          A        B        C        D        E        F        G        H
1
2
```

When you retrieve a file, 1-2-3 will always list all the .WK1 files on your data disk (*.WK1 means all files which have a .WK1 extension). You can then simply move the cursor to highlight the file you require and press Enter. This just saves you having to type the file name every time, with the possibility of typing it incorrectly and having to type it again.

As we only have one file on disk, QSALES.WK1 should be highlighted. If you press Enter the file should be loaded into the worksheet area.

If you saved your file with a password, when you press Enter the screen will go blank and you will be prompted to enter the password:

> *Type* **'Password' [Enter]**

Again, a small box will be displayed rather than the characters you type. However, if you get the password wrong, 1-2-3 will beep at you, the mode indicator will flash ERROR and you will be informed in the bottom left-hand corner of your screen that you have entered an incorrect password. You will need to press Escape to return you to the READY mode and start again.

Once you have successfully retrieved the file we are ready for the next section — printing.

■ SECTION 18
Printing the worksheet

Having possibly spent many hours preparing your worksheet it would be a shame to 'spoil' it by not taking care with the printing. Printing should not be a case of just feeding the paper into the printer and pressing Go to start. A little thought with regard to margins, headers, footers and titles can produce a professional looking printout suitable for the Bank Manager, Sales Director or Accountant.

For 1-2-3 the default page is made up as follows:

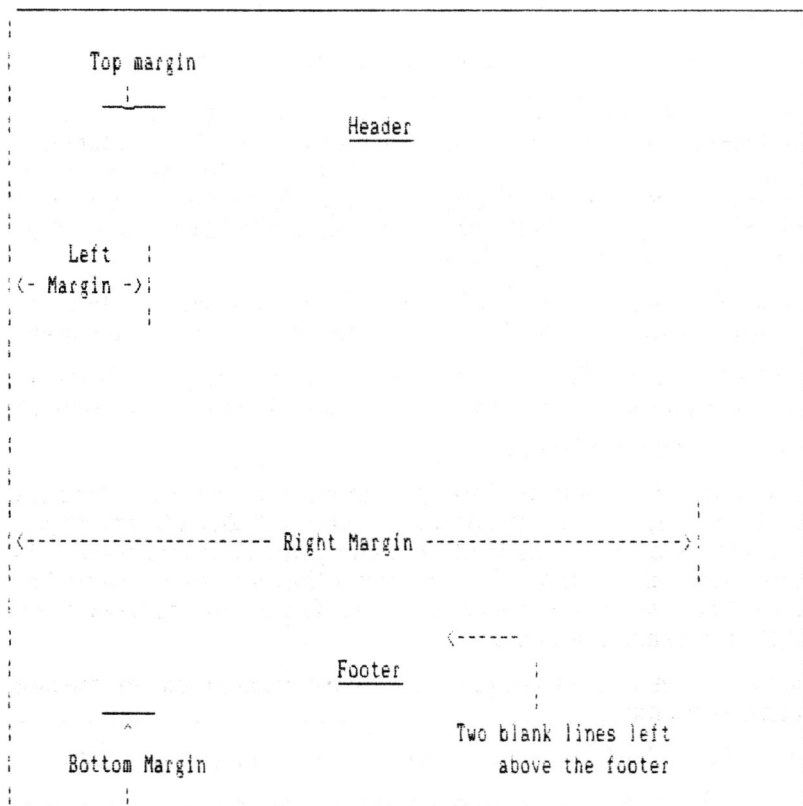

```
Top margin
      |

                              Header




   Left    |
|<- Margin ->|
   |         |







|<---------------------- Right Margin ---------------------->|


                      <------
                  Footer        |
      ___                       |
       ^                  Two blank lines left
   Bottom Margin             above the footer
```

■ SECTION 18
Printing the worksheet

The default page length is 66 lines of which you can print on 56 lines with the data from your worksheet as follows:

Lines 1 & 2	The top margin
Line 3	The header (or blank if no header specified)
Lines 4 & 5	*Blank*
Lines 6 – 61	Available to print lines from the worksheet
Lines 62 & 63	Blank
Line 64	The footer (or blank if no footer specified)
Lines 65 & 66	The bottom margin

You will have to determine the size of your paper and to set the margins to give a visually pleasing layout to your work. Whilst it all may seem a little complicated at first it is not quite as difficult as it first seems. Let's print out your worksheet to see how it is done.

First and foremost, make sure your printer is connected to the computer, it is switched on and there is paper in place.

With your QSALES worksheet on screen:

Type /
Type **P** to select **Print**
Type **P** to select **Printer**

The following menu will appear:

```
  A1:                                                      MENU
  Range  Line  Page  Options  Clear  Align  Go  Quit
  Specify a range to print
          A      B      C      D      E      F      G      H
  1
  2
```

Let's take each of these options in turn and see what they will do.

Range Specifies a range to print. Whilst you may at times find it a chore to identify the print range when you want the whole worksheet printing, you will find it very useful when you only require a portion of the worksheet to be printed.

Line Advances one line. This advances the paper one line at the printer.

Printing the worksheet

Page   Advances to top of page. This is similar to the Line command, but advances the paper one page length at the printer.

Options   These are as follows:

Header	Allows you to print one line of text up to 240 characters in length immediately below the top margin.
Footer	Allows you to print one line of text up to 240 characters in length immediately above the bottom margin (useful for page numbers).
Margins	Allows you to reset the left and right margins to a maximum of 240 and the top and bottom margins to a maximum of 32.
Borders	Allows you to specify rows or columns to be printed on every page. Row borders are printed above the range and column borders are printed to the left of the range you are printing.
Setup	Allows you to specify a printer setup string to enable your printer to print in a particular way. For example, entering \015 will cause the printer to print in condensed mode.
Pg-length	Allows you to set the number of lines per page and can be any length between 10 and 100.
Other	Allows you to print the worksheet as displayed, cell formulae, line by line, formatted or unformatted (suppresses headers, footers and page breaks).
Quit	Returns you to the print menu.

Clear   Allows you to reset some or all print settings.

Align   Resets the top of page after you have adjusted the paper. This essentially tells 1-2-3 where to start printing.

Go   Tells 1-2-3 to begin printing the specified range.

Quit   Returns you to the worksheet and READY mode.

First, we will set the range to be printed:

Type   **R** to select **Range**

■ SECTION 18
Printing the worksheet

You will be prompted to enter the print range and the current cell will be given as the starting point. If not already there:

Move the cursor to cell A1

Press the full-stop (or period) key

Move the cursor to cell G19 — note that the cells are highlighted as you go. All the cells, and only those cells, that you highlight will be printed.

Press Enter

You will be returned to the print menu and the range will be set.

Make sure the paper in the printer is ready for printing and that the printer is 'on line':

Type **A** to select **Align**

Type **G** to select **Go**

Your worksheet should now begin to be printed.

When you see the completed output you will be able to determine if the default settings suit your printer and your tastes. If not, reset the appropriate settings from the print menu until the printout is to your satisfaction.

Providing you follow the above procedure you should have no problems in producing professional looking output. Large worksheets sometimes cause a problem when they will not fit on your width of paper. There are several ways round this:

1 Leave the settings as they are and 1-2-3 will print your worksheet on two pages which can then be read side-by-side.

2 There are several programs on the market that will allow you to print spreadsheets sideways, i.e. the width of the worksheet is printed length-ways on the paper. (It is rumoured that the next release of 1-2-3 with have this function built-in.)

3 Print the worksheet in condensed mode by including the setup string, \015, but note you will need to adjust the right-hand margin to make 1-2-3 print the full width of the page.

Which method you choose is up to you and what you prefer. If possible, try all three and then make a decision as to which you like best.

PART FOUR

Graphical presentations

Introduction to graphs and charts

Many people have a natural aversion to numbers and have difficulty understanding the information they contain. To help overcome this problem, graphs and charts are used extensively to represent the numbers in a diagrammatical format. You will have noticed their use by the national press, magazines, journals and company report and accounts, In fact, anywhere it is desirable for the reader to be made aware of the significance of the numbers being discussed or analysed.

Lotus 1-2-3 allows you to create several different types of graph and chart. These are:

Line graphs — useful for showing trends in the data.

Bar charts — useful when making comparisons.

Stacked-bar charts — useful for comparing the component parts of various 'wholes'.

Pie charts — useful for showing the relationship of various parts which comprise a single 'whole'.

X-Y graphs — useful for establishing if a relationship exists between two variables or two sets of data.

When using the computer to draw graphs it is important that you make sure you understand which data you need to give the required outcome. It does no harm to sketch the graphs you want on a piece of paper first, to clarify what it is you are trying to achieve. There is nothing more misleading than an incorrectly structured graph.

With 1-2-3, all graphs are created from the **Graph** menu by identifying the data to be graphed as **data ranges**. Several graphs can be 'held' at the same time, but each graph must first be named. Graphs cannot be printed from the System disk. Consequently, they must be saved from the Graph menu and then printed using the Printgraph program.

The current graph settings and any named graphs will be automatically saved with the worksheet when it is saved to disk. You can then view any graphs you have created when you retrieve the worksheet in the future.

■ SECTION 20
Creating a line graph

In 1-2-3, all graphs are created through the Graph menu. To get this on screen:

Type /
Type **G** to select **Graph**

You should see:

```
: A1:                                                              MENU :
: Type  X  A  B  C  D  E  F  Reset  View  Save  Options  Name  Quit   :
: Set graph type                                                      :
:       A        B        C        D        E        F        G      H :
: 1                                                                    :
: 2                                                                    :
```

We are going to create a simple line graph of Total Revenue.

The default setting for graph type is the **Line** graph, so there is no need at this stage to actually select the type required. We can move straight on to identifying the data to be graphed.

In 1-2-3, six sets of data can be included in a single graph and are established using the letters A, B, C, D, E and F on the graph menu. We only require one data range (A), which will be the contents of cells B13 to E13 :

Type **A** to select the first data range

You will be prompted to enter the range:

Type **B13..E13** (or highlight the range) [**Enter**]

You will be returned to the Graph menu.

That's it. You have created your first 1-2-3 graph. You can have a look at it at any time using the View command from the Graph menu:

Type **V** to select **View**

On screen you should have:

Creating a line graph

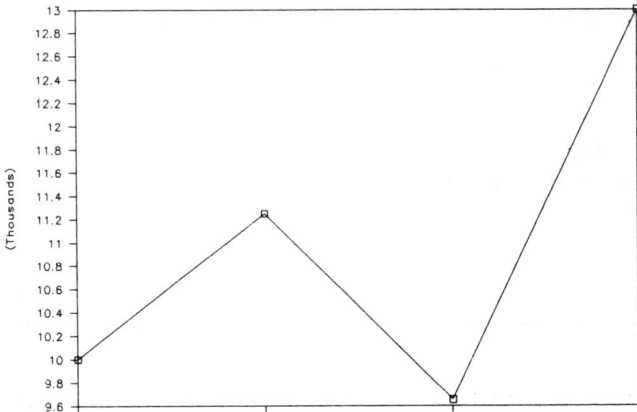

If you haven't, *re-select the appropriate option* and check you have highlighted the correct data range and amend if necessary. View the graph again by selecting the View option.

The graph very simply shows the revenue gained by the firm from the sales of all its products each quarter. It is noticeable, even from this simple line graph, that quarter three is a 'low' period for the firm and is perhaps something they would want to investigate further. (We will return to this problem when we create a bar chart in the next Section.) This could lead to the introduction of new products which would sell well at this time of year or an advertising campaign to stimulate the sales of existing products.

However, as it stands, the graph means very little since it is not labelled, does not indicate which data the line represents nor do we know what the axes are. The next step, then, is to assign various labels to the relevant parts of the graph. First, press any key to remove the graph and return to the graph menu.

Most of the labelling is carried out through the options menu:

    Type **O** to select **Options** from the Graph menu

■ SECTION 20
Creating a line graph

You should see the following at the top of your screen:

```
: A1:                                                           MENU :
: Legend  Format  Titles  Grid  Scale  Color  B&W  Data-Labels  Quit  :
: Specify data-range legends                                          :
:        B       C      D      E      F      G         H         I  : :
: 1                                                                  :
: 2                                                                  :
```

Here is a brief description of what can be done with each option:

■ **Legend** creates a key.

■ **Format** shows line graphs with lines, symbols, both or neither.

■ **Titles** provides two lines for a graph title to be entered and labels the X and Y axes.

■ **Grid** sets horizontal and/or vertical grid lines on your graph.

■ **Scale** provides for automatic or manual scaling of the axes.

■ **Color** allows you to determine how the graph is shown in colour if you have a colour monitor.

■ **B&W** displays the graph in black and white.

■ **Data-Labels** places a label corresponding to a value on the graph.

■ **Quit** returns you to the Graph menu.

We will use several of these options throughout this book but it is recommended that you experiment with the different options available so that you can create the type of graph that *you* want.

Creating a line graph

To add a title

The title of any graph is most important and should succinctly explain what the graph shows. You must remember that whilst it is obvious to you now, it will not be in a few months' time and other people who may see the graph would not have a clue unless you state it clearly with a good title. Think carefully before you type, though it can be amended later if necessary.

If you have not already done so, to leave the view of the graph and return to the Graph menu press any key.

Type **O** to select **Options**
Type **T** to select **Titles**

You will be given the choice of:

First   Second   X-axis   Y-axis

Type **F** to select the **First line**
Type **Total Revenue on a Quarterly Basis [Enter]**
Type **T** again
Type **S** to select the **Second line**
Type **All Products – 1987 [Enter]**

You can view the graph again by pressing the Escape key or Q for Quit to take you out of the Options menu and back to the Graph menu and then pressing V for View.

Creating a line graph

To label the axes

In 1-2-3 the convention is followed that the X axis runs horizontally and the Y axis runs vertically. Thus, the X axis of our graph records the time element (quarters of the year) which corresponds with what we said about planning and designing the worksheet with the columns to represent the quarters and rows to represent the products. In statistical terms, the X axis records the **independent variable** (the variable we have no control over) and the Y axis records the **dependent variable** (in this case, the level of Sales depends upon the time of year).

From the Graph menu:

Type **O**
Type **T**
Type **X** to select **X-axis**
Type **Quarters [Enter]**
Type **T** again
Type **Y** to select **Y-axis**
Type **£'s [Enter]**

Press Escape or Q for Quit to return to the Graph menu and view the graph to check your progress.

■ SECTION 20
Creating a line graph

To label the data

The individual values for the total revenue gained in each quarter should now be labelled on the X-axis so that they can be readily identified as being made in quarter 1, 2, 3 or 4:

Type **X** at the Graph menu

You will be prompted to enter the range. The labels we require, Q1, Q2, Q3 and Q4, are located in cells B5, C5, D5 and E5. So, instead of having to type these labels we simply highlight the range B5 to E5 and 1-2-3 will 'transfer' them from the worksheet on to the graph.

Move the cursor to B5
Press the full-stop key to anchor the range
Move the cursor to highlight B5 to E5 and then press Enter

Type **V** if you wish to view the graph at this stage.

Your Line graph is now finished and should look like this when you press V to view:

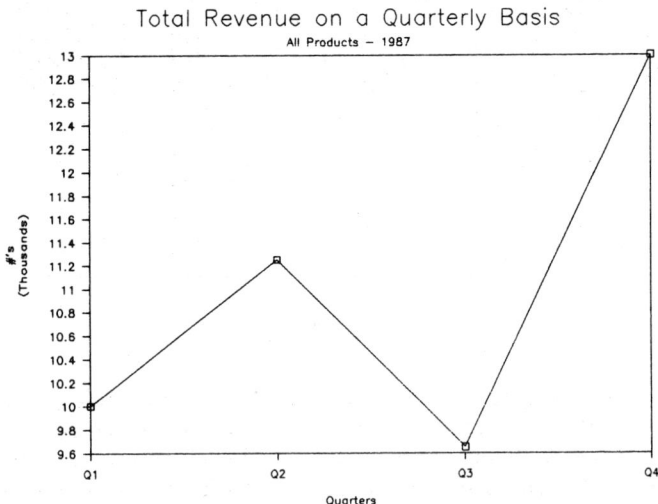

Total Revenue on a Quarterly Basis
All Products — 1987

If you notice any typing errors in your titles or labels, simply *reselect the appropriate option* and edit the entry.

74

■ SECTION 21
The bar chart

The bar chart is created using exactly the same principles as used for the line graph.

We have already identified one data range (data range A) and incorporated labels into the graph. We can use them to display the same information, but in the bar chart format.

Type **T** to select **Type of graph**
Type **B** to select **Bar chart**
Type **V** to select **View**

Your graph should have been changed to a simple bar chart which looks like this:

Total Revenue on a Quarterly Basis
All Products — 1987

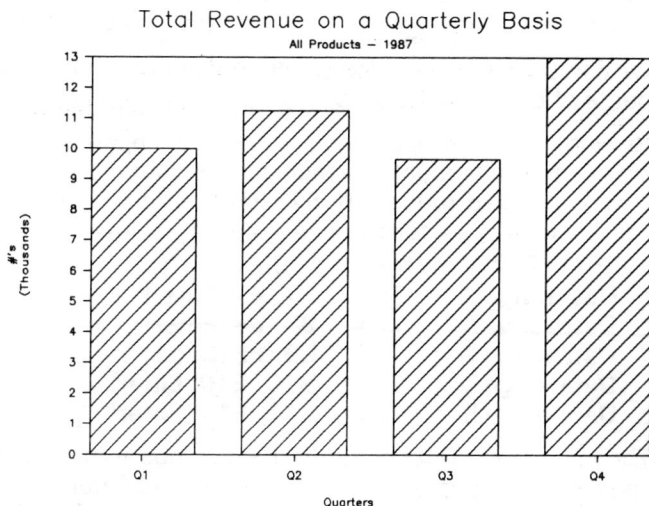

By simply pressing two keys you have transformed the information into a completely different format and all your work in creating labels has not been lost. This is particularly useful when you are uncertain which type of graph will best suit your needs or where you wish to show several aspects of the same data in different ways. But let us see how we would change the settings to create a bar chart of different areas of the worksheet.

■ SECTION 21
The bar chart

Naming the graph settings

Where you intend to create more than one graph from the same data you must first **Name** the current graph so that the settings will be retained by 1-2-3. To return to our original line graph we simply reselect the graph type to Line:

Type **T**
Type **L**

We will name the graph Revenue:

Type **N** to select **Name**
Type **C** to select **Create**
Type **Revenue [Enter]**

The settings for the line graph will now be stored by 1-2-3 for future use and we can confidently proceed to create a bar chart that employs other aspects of the worksheet data.

An interesting chart would be one that compares the sales 'performance' of each product – a multiple bar chart. As there are five products, we will need to identify five data ranges. This is done in exactly the same way as for the line graph by selecting each data range in turn and entering the following:

Select	**Data range A**	*Type*	**B7..E7 [Enter]**
Select	**Data range B**	*Type*	**B8..E8 [Enter]**
Select	**Data range C**	*Type*	**B9..E9 [Enter]**
Select	**Data range D**	*Type*	**B10..E10 [Enter]**
Select	**Data range E**	*Type*	**B11..E11 [Enter]**

Note   When you select Data range A, the previous settings of B13 to E13 are highlighted. Simply type B7..E7 and press Enter to establish the new data range we require for the bar chart. Don't forget also to change the graph type to **Bar.**

The bar chart

When you have entered the data ranges, view the bar chart. It should look like this:

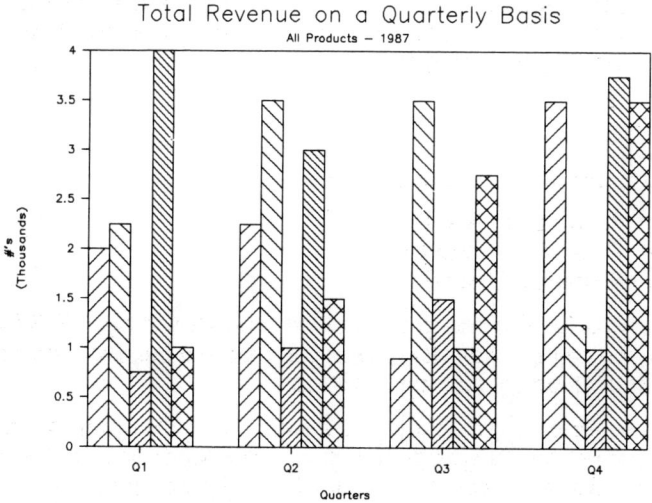

Total Revenue on a Quarterly Basis
All Products — 1987

Notice all your labels are still intact and can be used, if appropriate, or amended as necessary by selecting the appropriate Option and editing the offending label.

First, the title is no longer appropriate:

Type	**O**
Type	**T**
Type	**F**
Type	**Esc** to cancel the full line
Type	**Quarterly Sales By Product [Enter]**

The second line of the title does not need amending, but whilst we are in the Options menu we will create a key to explain the significance of the shading of the bars. With 1-2-3, a key is created using the option **Legend**:

Type   **L** to select **Legend**

You will be prompted to select a data range (A to F) to create a key:

Type   **A** to select the **first data range**
Type   **P1 [Enter]**

You will be returned to the Options menu with Legend highlighted. You now need to repeat the process for each data range contained in the bar chart, A to E, and typing P2, P3, P4 and P5 for the appropriate range.

The successful conclusion to your endeavours should be:

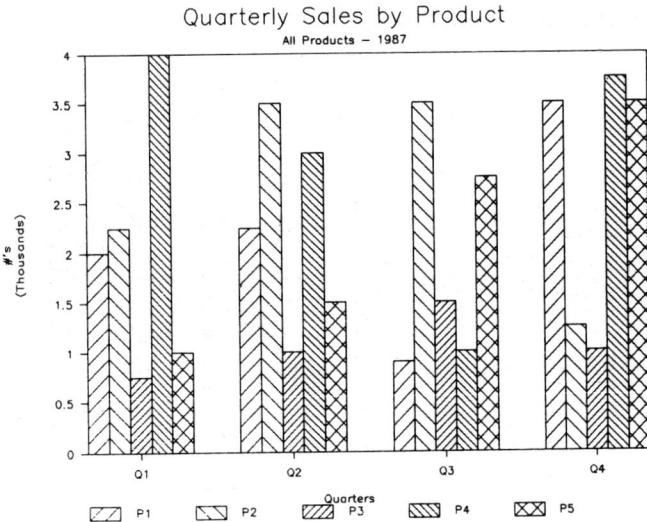

If you spot any differences, simply amend the entry by selecting the appropriate option and edit the entry until you are satisfied all is correct.

You should now **Name** the bar chart so that 1-2-3 will store the settings for future use.

May I suggest **BSALES**. (The B just stands for Bar chart and will allow us to distinguish it from the stacked-bar chart we will create in the next Section.)

The stacked-bar chart

The stacked-bar chart or component bar chart as it is often called, is an alternative view of exactly the same data used for the bar chart. All we need to do is change the graph type from the Graph menu:

Type   **T** to select **Type of graph**
Type   **S** to select **Stacked-bar**
Type   **V** to **View**

On screen you should now have:

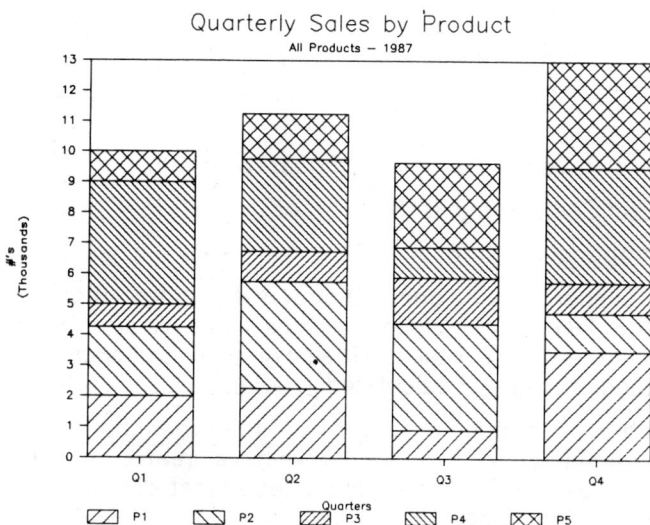

Quarterly Sales by Product
All Products – 1987

The stacked-bar chart can be quite difficult to read, especially when there are many components to each bar. However, it does have one distinct advantage over other types of graphs and charts and that is its ability to easily indicate the changing ratio of the various components that comprise each bar. If you study the chart on screen, you should notice in particular the changing contribution to total sales made by:

Product 1 in Quarter 3
Product 4 in Quarter 3
Product 2 in Quarter 4
Product 5 in Quarter 1

Before moving on to the next Section, you should **Name** the graph settings. A graph name of **SBSALES** would nicely distinguish this chart from the bar chart named in the previous Section.

■ SECTION 23
The pie chart

This is one of the most popular means of displaying figures in chart form. It has good visual impact, particularly when one or more 'slices' are 'exploded' from the main body. However, it must be treated with a certain amount of care. The pie chart identifies the individual component parts of a single whole and displays them in the form of a circle, the size of the circle representing the value of the whole.

Consequently, the pie chart can only ever comprise one data range.

Much of the data in our worksheet is suitable for pie charts since it comprises many individual numbers added together to obtain totals. We could, for example, create pie charts showing:

■   The quarterly sales totals (using the range B7..B11, or C7..C11, etc.).

■   The Total Revenue (using the range B13..E13).

■   The Total Costs (range B16..E16), or

■   Profit (range B18..C18).

A more useful chart may be one that shows the contribution of each product to the Yearly Total. Since the slices of the pie are determined by their percentage of the total, it will also give you a chance to check the percentages that 1-2-3 calculated in column G.

As the pie chart is so much different from the other charts (and the fact that by naming each of the graphs we have created so far means we can recall those settings at anytime), let's reset all graph settings and start with a clean 'sheet'.

From the Graph menu:

Type   R to select **Reset**
Type   G to select **Graph**

All the settings, including the axes labels, titles and key will be erased and we are ready to produce a pie chart.

First, select the type of graph:

Type   **T**
Type   P to select **Pie**

The one data range we require for a pie chart is normally identified using data range A:

Type   A to select the data range
Type   F7..F11 (or highlight the range)[**Enter**]

■ SECTION 23
The pie chart

The pie chart has now been created and if you view it, you should see:

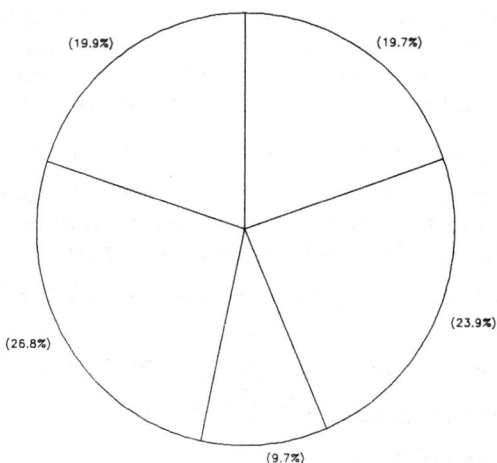

You will agree that this is not a particularly inspiring pie chart, but we will substantially improve it shortly. First, just run a quick check on the percentages shown on the pie chart with those calculated by your worksheet. They should be the same. (They *must* be the same or else your worksheet formulae are incorrect or you have identified the wrong range for the pie chart!)

Press any key to leave the view of the pie chart and we will see how we can improve its appearance.

It will not be obvious why at the moment, but:

Type **B** to select **Data range B**
Type **I7..I11** [**Enter**]

Now, Quit the Graph menu to return to the worksheet READY mode as we need to enter some numbers in cells I7 to I11 which you have just designated as data range B:

Type **101** in I7
Type **2** in I8
Type **3** in I9
Type **4** in I10
Type **5** in I11

■ SECTION 23
The pie chart

Locate **function key F10**: this is the **Graph** key and allows you to view the current graph at any time whilst you are in READY mode. This is useful when you are creating a pie chart as you will see in a moment. But, more importantly, you can instantly see the effect of any changes you make to the worksheet by viewing the graph. (See Section on Break-even Analysis for a particularly good case in point.)

If you press F10, the effect on your pie chart should be quite startling, for it should appear thus:

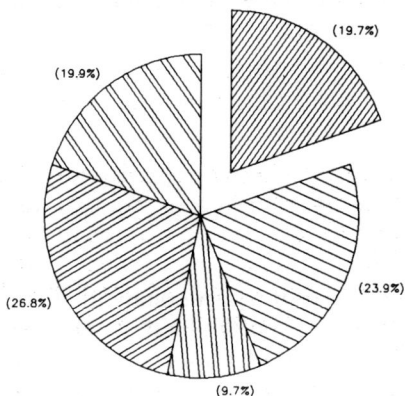

Look at what has happened. By adding numbers to the cells you identified as data range B, each slice has been shaded and the slice representing the sales of Product 1 has been 'exploded' from the rest of the pie. Very impressive. The secret lies in the numbers you enter for data range B.

■ SECTION 23
The pie chart

■ Seven different patterns can be used for shading, the appropriate numbers being 1 to 7.

■ The numbers 0 and 8 are also available to leave a slice with no shading.

■ A slice is 'exploded' by adding 100 to the shading code. In the example you have just done you allocated a shading code of 1 to Product 1, added 100 to make it 'explode' giving the number 101 to be entered in cell I7.

Note The codes must be placed in a row or column corresponding to the data the shading will represent.

Now, you may not like the shadings I have allocated to each slice so you can change them by simply entering a new shading code in the appropriate cell.

The slice of pie you want to 'explode' will depend on which value or product you wish to draw attention to. For example, you might wish to highlight the product that has contributed most to the yearly total (Product 4), the product that has contributed least to the yearly total (Product 3), a product that has recently been added to the range or a product that has been the subject of a 'special offer' campaign throughout the year.

Using the Graph key (**F10**) you can view the outcome, make more amendments if necessary and view the pie chart again without having to leave the worksheet READY mode. You can very quickly and very easily experiment until you get just the right pie chart you are looking for.

But now we must return to the Graph menu so that we can add the various titles and labels that make the pie chart mean something to all who see it:

Type /
Type **G** to select **Graph**

The pie chart

To label the slices

The X on the Graph menu is used to label the individual slices. We do not have to type each label but simply specify the range of cells in which they appear in the worksheet:

Type **X**
Type **A7..A11** (or highlight the range) **[Enter]**

You should now enter the title and axes labels as you have done previously. If you have used the same shading, etc., as I have, your completed pie chart should look like this:

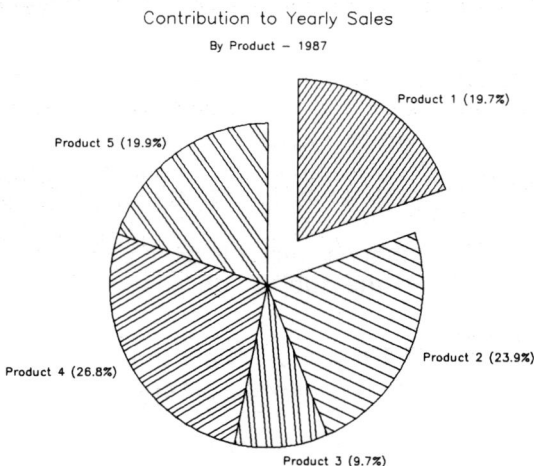

Contribution to Yearly Sales

By Product — 1987

Product 1 (19.7%)

Product 5 (19.9%)

Product 2 (23.9%)

Product 4 (26.8%)

Product 3 (9.7%)

If it doesn't, remember you can reselect the appropriate option and make any amendments that are necessary.

You should now **Name** the pie chart from the Graph menu so that it can be recalled in the future. Use the Reset option to clear the pie chart settings once they have been named and we will proceed to create an X-Y graph.

■ SECTION 24
The X-Y graph

The X-Y graph is a 'special' graph which shows the relationship (if any) between two variables. For example, you may wish to know if there is a relationship between the amount of expenditure undertaken on advertising and the level of sales (hopefully yes) and if there is, how strong is it?

The X-Y graph plots pairs of values on to one graph and joins each point with a continuous line. The straighter the line the stronger is the relationship between the two variables. If the line slopes upwards there is said to be a positive relationship. A negative relationship exists if the resulting line slopes downwards.

Let's see if there is a relationship between Total Revenue and Total Costs.

Note You should have named the pie chart and reset the graph settings in the previous section. If you have not already done so, do so now.

The independent variable, Total Revenue, will be plotted along the X axis and Total Cost (the dependent variable) along the Y axis.
   When creating an X-Y graph, X is used as a data range **not** to identify labels as with other graphs. From the Graph menu:

Type   **X**
Type   **B13..E13** (or highlight the range [**Enter**])
Type   **A**
Type   **B16..E16** (or highlight the range) [**Enter**]

You can now add the titles and label the axes as you have done previously using Options from the Graph menu. Whilst your title and axes labels may be somewhat different to mine, generally the completed graph should look like this:

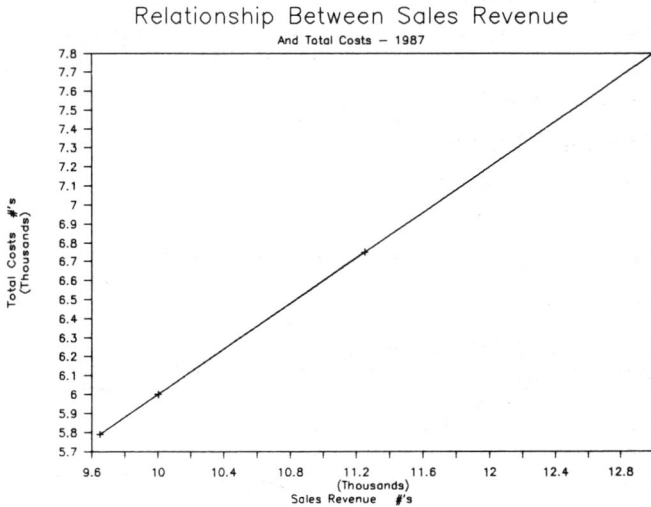

Relationship Between Sales Revenue
And Total Costs — 1987

As you can see, and probably expected, there is a strong relationship between Total Revenue and Total Cost. In fact, there is a direct relationship between the two. For some types of businesses this will be true if you looked at perhaps, the Gross Margin of Sales to Cost of Sales. If you can establish that this is approximately true for your business, you can build the information into the worksheet to improve its operation. We will return to this point when we look at cash-flow forecasts in Section 26.

■ SECTION 25
Printing your graphs and charts

Graphs and charts can not be printed directly from the System disk as we did with the worksheet. It is necessary to first save the graphs to disk, exit from the spreadsheet and load in the **Printgraph** program.

Saving graphs for printing

Each graph you want to print out *must be saved from the Graph menu.* If you want to print all the graphs you have created in the previous sections, you will need to follow this procedure:

1   Make the graph current:

> *Type* **N** to select **Name**
> *Type* **U** to select **Use**

Highlight the graph name and then press Enter.

2   Save the graph:

> *Type* **S** to select **Save**
> *Type* An appropriate file name, maximum eight characters and no file extension
> *Type* [**Enter**]

3   Repeat steps 1 and 2 for each graph you want to print.

It is important that you do not add a file extension to the graph name – 1-2-3 automatically adds the extension .PIC to all graph files and will look for this extension when you come to print the graph.

The Printgraph disk

You will remember that during the installation procedure when you told 1-2-3 the type of equipment you have, that certain information was saved to your Printgraph disk. This was mainly the details of the graphics printer(s) you have connected to the computer so that an appropriate driver could be loaded into the 1-2-3 driver set. Providing you followed the Install procedure, you will experience no problems in printing out your graphs.

The Printgraph program can be started either from the Install System:

> Highlight **Printgraph**
> *Type* [**Enter**]
> Insert Printgraph disk in drive A when requested to do so.
> *Type* [**Enter**]

Printing your graphs and charts

or from the DOS A> prompt:

Insert the **Printgraph** disk in drive A
Type **pgraph** [**Enter**]

After the 1-2-3 logo and copyright notice, the printgraph screen will appear like this:

```
:Copyright 1985 Lotus Development Corp. All Rights Reserved. Release 2 MENU:

:
:
: Select graphs for printing
: Image-Select  Settings  Go  Align  Page  Exit

:
:    GRAPH     IMAGE OPTIONS                    HARDWARE SETUP
:    IMAGES      Size            Range Colors     Graphs Directory:
:    SELECTED    Top      .395   X Black            B:\
:                Left     .750   A Black          Fonts Directory:
:                Width   6.500   B Black            A:\
:                Height  4.691   C Black          Interface:
:                Rotate   .000   D Black            Parallel 1
:                               E Black          Printer Type:
:                Font           F Black            Epson FX.RX/Lo
:                1  BLOCK1                        Paper Size
:                2  BLOCK1                          Width      8.500
:                                                  Length    11.000

:                                                ACTION OPTIONS
:                                                  Pause: No   Eject: No
:
```

As you can see, there are several settings you can select (which will affect the appearance of your graphs) as well as hardware changes that you can make. In my case, some of the options are not available to me because of the equipment I own (or rather do not own). For example, the range of colours available to me comprises black since I do not possess a plotter that will print in colour and the paper size is limited by the printer I own.

Printing your graphs and charts

The **Settings** option gives the following submenu:

Image   Allows you to specify size, fonts and colours.

Size   Can be:

   Full page layout which sets rotation to 90 degrees to print the graph sideways. Printgraph sets the height and width values automatically.

   Half page layout sets rotation to 0 degrees, the height and width values are set automatically and two graphs can be printed per page.

Manual   Lets you set all the variables, i.e. the top and bottom margins, the width of the graph and the height of the graph all in inches, and the number of degrees the graph is to be rotated anti-clockwise (90 degrees produces a quarter turn to the left).

Fonts   Determines the typeface for the text portions of the graph. Several fonts are available including bold, italic and roman and a full list will be presented to you for you to select from.

Colours   The range of colours allowed by your printer or plotter can be assigned to the ranges (A to F) used by your graph. The X range is used to determine the colour of the box that contains the graph and everything outside the box except the key.

Hardware   Allows you to specify various aspects of your equipment.

Graphs directory   The drive where Printgraph will search for your graph files, i.e. those with the .PIC extension.

Fonts directory   The drive where Printgraph will search for font styles.

Interface   To determine the type and number of printers connected to your system.

Printer   To select the appropriate printer from the list you selected with the Install program.

Size-paper   Identifies the size of the paper in inches used by your printer.

Action   Allows you to determine what happens between the printing of graphs.

Pause   Selecting Yes causes Printgraph to pause between the printing of each graph and beeps so that you can change paper or adjust settings on your printer.

Eject   Selecting Yes causes Printgraph to advance the paper to the next page after each graph is printed.

Save Allows you to save any changes you have made in Settings so that you start Printgraph each time with the new settings.

Reset Replaces any changes you have just made with the settings previously stored to disk.

To print a graph

Type I to select **Image-select**

A list of the graph files you have created will appear on screen with a set of instructions of how to proceed. All the files listed here will have the .PIC extension.

Note Only those files saved from the Graph menu and having the .PIC extension can be printed by Printgraph.

First, you must select the graph(s) to be printed from the list of those available. Do this by moving the cursor key to highlight the graph you want to print. To check if this is the right graph, press **F10** and the graph will be displayed on screen. Press any key to return to the list of files.

Type **space bar** to mark (or unmark) your selection
Type [**Enter**]

You will be returned to the menu.

Make sure your printer is switched on and is 'on line':

Type **A** to select **Align paper**
Type **G** to select **Go**

You can now sit back whilst the graph is printed. This will take a little time depending on the complexity of your graph, so be patient.

■ SECTION 25
Printing your graphs and charts

You can, of course, print several graphs one after the other by marking each of them with the space bar. If you are using continuous stationery, then Printgraph will automatically advance the paper when required, assuming you have set Action correctly from the **Hardware settings** option.

Now that you can see the graph on paper, you may be dissatisfied with the default settings offered by 1-2-3. You should experiment with different margins, widths and heights until you arrive at a format that suits you. Be sure you have plenty of time available for this exercise because each graph does take a little time to be printed. You will, however, be rewarded with very nice presentations of your work, which is worth waiting for.

PART FIVE

Financial applications

■ SECTION 26
Coping with larger worksheets

So far, all the work you have done has been nicely contained within the boundaries of your monitor screen, making it easy to see what is going on throughout the whole model. It is inevitable that sooner or later the worksheet you are creating will be too large to fit on one screen; the cash-flow forecast in the next section is a good example. Here are a few tips for making large worksheets easier to live with.

Locking the titles

The first problem you will encounter is the row and column headings disappearing off the screen as you scroll through the worksheet. To lock the titles in position so that they are on view all the time:

1   Place the cursor *immediately below and immediately to the right of* the labels you wish to lock into position. This would be cell B7 in the cash-flow forecast shown in the next section.

2   *Type* */*
    Type **W**
    Type **T** to select **Titles**

3   The following selection will be displayed:

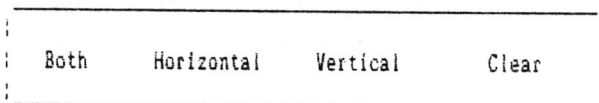

```
    Both      Horizontal     Vertical        Clear
```

4   *Type* **B** to select **Both**

5   You will be returned to the READY mode.

You can now move around any part of the worksheet and your row and column headings will always be in view. You will find that this helps to make sure you enter the correct figures in their correct locations.

■ SECTION 26
Coping with larger worksheets

Creating windows

Another useful feature of 1-2-3 is the ability to split the screen into two windows, either vertically or horizontally. This is particularly useful when you experiment with 'What if?' tests at the top of the worksheet, but you want to see the effect on the contents of a cell that is not on the screen. By creating windows you can manipulate the worksheet so that the cells you are interested in can be on the screen at the same time. This is done in the following manner:

1   Place the cursor in the row or column where you want the window to be created, i.e. the row will become the top edge of a horizontal window and the column will become the left edge of a vertical window.

2   *Type* **/**
     Type **W** to select **Worksheet**
     Type **W** to select **Windows**

3   You will be given the following options:

Horizontal	Vertical	Sync	Unsync	Clear

Brief details of the effect of selecting each of the windows options are given below:

Horizontal, as you would expect, creates two windows with the screen split horizontally.

Vertical creates two windows with the screen split vertically.

Sync stands for synchronised movement of the contents of each window. With *horizontal windows* this means that as you scroll through one window horizontally, the other window also scrolls, keeping the *same columns* on screen in both windows. With *vertical windows* this means that as you scroll through one window vertically, the other window also scrolls vertically, keeping the *same rows* on screen in both windows.

Unsync stands for unsynchronised movement of the contents of each window and means that the windows will scroll *independently*.

■ SECTION 26
Coping with larger worksheets

Clear removes the second window from the screen and returns you to a normal screen.

F6 (function key F6) toggles (switches) the cursor between the two windows you have created.

Whilst in either window, the 1-2-3 functions, commands and operations are exactly the same as if you were working on the normal screen.

When manipulating large worksheets you can make good use of some of the keys mentioned in Section 7. In particular, you should find that **F5**, the Goto key, and the **End** key in conjunction with a **cursor** key can speed up movement around the worksheet quite significantly.

Depending on the size of your worksheet, **Big left**, **Big right**, **PgUp** and **PgDn** may be useful, particularly if your worksheet is contained in two 'screenfuls'.

■ SECTION 26
Coping with larger worksheets

Manual recalculation

Each time an entry is made in the worksheet, 1-2-3 recalculates the whole worksheet automatically. With large worksheets this can take several seconds which soon becomes irritating if you are waiting to make another entry.

Automatic recalculation can be turned off using the following sequence of commands:

Type /
Type **W** to select **Worksheet**
Type **G** to select **Global**
Type **R** to select **Recalculation**
Type **M** to select **Manual**

You will be returned to the READY mode.

You will find this can speed up the entry of data quite significantly.

Once you make an entry into the worksheet having set Manual recalculation, 1-2-3 will remind you of the fact by displaying the word **Calc** at the bottom right-hand side of your screen. I view this as a warning that the results of the formulae contained within the model must be updated by pressing the **Calc** key (**F9**).

To return to automatic recalculation simply select Automatic from the Recalculation menu:

Type /
Type **W** to select **Worksheet**
Type **G** to select **Global**
Type **R** to select **Recalculation**
Type **A** to select **Automatic**

You will be returned to the READY mode.

If the **Calc** indicator is still displayed, press **F9**.

The cash-flow forecast

Many businesses, particularly small ones, could avoid cash-flow problems by using a cash-flow forecast to monitor their performance. No one can forecast the future accurately, but you will find that it is only necessary to have some figures to guide you in order to prevent short-term cash problems.

When incorporated in a business plan, the cash-flow forecast is an indispensable asset in convincing your bank manager to lend you money or provide overdraft facilities. This is not to say the loan or overdraft facility will be granted automatically, but a well presented case will offer you the best chance of success.

The forecast, however, should not just be presented to the bank manager and then forgotten about. Using the worksheet you have set up to monitor your performance on a monthly basis provides you with a certain amount of control of your business. By comparing forecast figures with actual results you can ask yourself why certain costs have increased or is there a reason why the sales were not achieved in a particular month. Knowing the specific areas where things have gone wrong makes it easier to make decisions on what is required to put things right.

With 1-2-3 it is also easy to test 'What if?' situations and immediately see the effect it will have on your overall trading position. What happens if you buy a new piece of equipment? What happens if you take on a particular contract? What is the effect of negotiating a longer period in which to pay suppliers? As a consequence, you can anticipate the problems or benefits and take action accordingly.

The sample cash-flow forecast shown on the following pages is quite complicated, but has been created with the basic skills developed in the previous sections. The figures relate to a small garage that derives its income from two activities: undertaking repairs of motor vehicles and selling petrol.

The forecast assumes that all petrol is sold for cash and that customers pay for repairs the month after they were carried out. Purchases of both spare parts and petrol are on two months' credit, i.e. are paid for two months after they are received by the garage.

It has also been estimated that spare parts cost approximately 60% of the revenue received from repairs and that petrol costs 75% of sales.

Other costs such as wages, electricity, rent and rates have been identified, estimated and included in the forecast under Expenditures.

The main thing to remember with cash-flow forecasts is that they record cash *as and when* it comes into or leaves the firm. Consequently, you will notice that no income is generated in the first month from repairs because the garage will not be paid until the following month. (This assumes that the garage was not trading in the previous year.)

You will also notice that two additional columns have been created to the right of the table. This is not part of the main cash-flow forecast and would not, for example, be printed out for presentation to your bank manager. However, you will find it extremely useful when we come to produce a projected Profit and Loss Account in Section 28.

The cash-flow printout is shown overleaf.

Entering the model

Much of the data in the cash-flow forecast is entered straight from the keyboard. However, there is also a liberal sprinkling of formulae, all of which you have met before.

Total Income is calculated in cell B12 by the formula +B9+B10, which can be copied to cells C12..M12.

Total Expenditure is calculated in cell B29 by the formula @SUM(B18..B27) and can be copied to cells C29..M29.

The **Totals** column contains a similar formula, @SUM(B9..M9), which can be copied to the appropriate cells in that column.

Since it has been established that purchases are approximately equal to a percentage of the income they generate, a formula has been included for both petrol and repairs.

Nothing will appear in cells B18, C18, B19 or C19 as purchases are obtained on two months' credit. (This assumes the garage was not trading 'last year').

The formula in D18 is +C9*0.6 (which can be copied to cells E18..M18) and in D19 is +B10*0.75 (which can be copied to cells E19..M19). Both these formulae take the value of sales and multiply by the appropriate decimal to give the required value of purchases. The difficulty arises in matching the right sales to the right purchases. In the case of petrol, this is reasonably straightforward. The sales for January are estimated to be £2000 and the cost of buying this petrol (75% of £2000) has to be met two months later in March.

A1: [W15] 'CASH FLOW FORECAST - Jan to Dec 1988

	A	B	C	D	E	F	G	H
1	CASH FLOW FORECAST - Jan to Dec 1988							
2								
3								
4								
5		Jan	Feb	Mar	Apr	May	June	July
6								
7	INCOME							
8								
9	Repairs		6100	6250	6950	7250	9050	9850
10	Petrol	2000	2000	2100	2500	2750	3500	3500
11	-------							
12	Total Income	2000	8100	8350	9450	10000	12550	13350
13	-------							
14								
15	EXPENDITURE							
16								
17	Purchases:							
18	Spare-parts			3660	3750	4170	4350	5430
19	Petrol			1500	1500	1575	1875	2062.5
20	Wages	2000	2000	2000	2000	2000	2000	2000
21	Electricity			500			500	
22	Rent	600	600	600	600	600	600	600
23	Rates						500	
24	Telephone			150			150	
25	Postage	20	20	20	20	20	20	20
26	Accountant							
27	Sundries	20	20	20	20	20	20	20
28	-------							
29	Total Expend	2640	2640	8450	7890	8385	10015	10132.5
30	-------							
31								
32	NET CASH FLOW	-640	5460	-100	1560	1615	2535	3217.5
33	Opening Balance	2000	1360	6820	6720	8280	9895	12430
34	Closing Balance	1360	6820	6720	8280	9895	12430	15647.5
35								

H	I	J	K	L	M	N	O	P
							Adjustments	
July	Aug	Sept	Oct	Nov	Dec	TOTAL	1	2
9850	10100	9150	8160	7000	5500	85360	4300	
3500	2750	2600	2100	2000	2500	30300		
-------	-------	-------	-------	-------	-------	-------		
13350	12850	11750	10260	9000	8000	115660		
-------	-------	-------	-------	-------	-------	-------		
5430	5910	6060	5490	4896	4200	47916	3300	2580
2062.5	2625	2625	2062.5	1950	1575	19350	1500	1875
2000	2000	2000	2000	2000	2000	24000		
		500			500	2000		
600	600	600	600	600	600	7200		
					500	1000		
		150			150	600		
20	20	20	20	20	20	240		
					450	450		
20	20	20	20	20	20	240		
-------	-------	-------	-------	-------	-------	-------		
10132.5	11175	11975	10192.5	9486	10015	102996		
-------	-------	-------	-------	-------	-------	-------		
3217.5	1675	-225	67.5	-486	-2015			
12430	15647.5	17322.5	17097.5	17165	16679			
15647.5	17322.5	17097.5	17165	16679	14664			

The cash-flow forecast

Consequently, the formula takes the value in cell B10 (the sales of petrol), multiplies it by 0.75 and displays the result under the March heading in cell D19, when the petrol has to be paid for.

Repairs are a little more complicated, but follow the same principles. The repairs undertaken in January are not paid for until February (C9) and the parts must be paid for in March. Consequently, the formula takes the value in C9 (the cell in which payment is received for the *January* repairs), multiplies it by 0.6 and displays the result under the March heading in cell D18, when the spare parts have to be paid for.

The adjustment columns record the income not yet received from repairs and purchases not yet paid for.

The income figure is typed in cell O9 from the keyboard.

The purchases columns contain formulae that are similar to those in the main body of the cash-flow:

  Cell O18 contains +M9*0.6
  Cell O19 contains +L10*0.75
  Cell P18 contains +O9*0.6
  Cell P19 contains +M10*0.75

Rows 32, 33 and 34 also warrant some explanation. The Net Cash Flow is simply the difference between Total Income and Total Expenditure and is calculated by +B12−B29 which can be copied to cells C32..M32.

The opening balance for January (recorded in cell B33) is typed from the keyboard corresponding with the information given.

The closing balance in cell B34 is the result of adding the opening balance to the net cash flow. The formula is +B33+B32 and can be copied to cells C34..M34.

The opening balances for February to December are based on the fact that the current month's opening balance is the previous month's closing balance. Consequently, cell C33 contains the formula +B34 (the cell address of the previous month's closing balance) and this can be copied to cells D33..M33.

The resultant figure in cell M34 is the amount that the garage can expect to have at the end of the year if all the figures are realised.

The cash-flow forecast

'What if?' tests

The model above makes as much use of formulae as possible. The main advantage of this (other than the accuracy of totals) is that changing a single item of data will be reflected throughout the whole worksheet.

You could test out various scenarios for your company and see the effect on your cash-flow. A 'favourable' test could induce you to set various targets for income and/or expenditure which could be monitored on a month-by-month basis. An 'unfavourable' test might prompt you to monitor various aspects of your business a little more closely.

Actual data could replace the forecast data once it is known. This would make it possible, for example, to anticipate the need for overdraft facilities in the short term so that you could make an appointment to see your bank manager post-haste.

As mentioned in Section 25, you will find it helpful to create a window so that you can observe on the screen the particular aspect of the forecast in which you are interested and the cell in which you are changing individual items of data.

Expanding the model

Each month could be assigned two columns, one for the forecast data and one for actual data. This would create quite a large worksheet and you may like to try this over six months at a time rather than a full year. With this set-up, you could monitor the performance of your business on a month by month basis by entering the actual data as soon as it is known. Any discrepancies between forecast and actual will be highlighted by comparing the two columns and enable you to take appropriate action where necessary.

Projected Profit & Loss Account

```
Q1:                                                        READY

         Q    R    S      T      U      V      W      X      Y
 1                    PROJECTED PROFIT & LOSS ACCOUNT
 2                            1988
 3
 4                                  £             £
 5              Revenue:
 6              Repairs                        89660
 7               Petrol                        30300
 8                                            --------
 9              Total Revenue                  119960
10
11              Less Purchases                 76521
12                                            --------
13              GROSS PROFIT                   43439
14
15
16              Less Expenditure
17
18              Wages            24000
19              Electricity       2000
20              Rent              7200
21              Rates             1000
22              Telephone          600
23              Postage            240
24              Accountant         450
25              Sundries           240        35730
26                               -----        --------
27
28              NET PROFIT/LOSS                 7709
29                                            ========
30
```

Projected Profit & Loss Account

Using the figures we have in the cash-flow forecast, we can produce a projected Profit & Loss Account for the business by using cell addresses and simple formulae for additions and subtractions.

First we need a suitable layout. In line with popular practice, I have used the standard vertical format for the Profit & Loss Account, the completed account being shown opposite.

You will notice that all the Income and Expenditure labels that appeared in the cash-flow forecast also appear in the Profit & Loss account. It is thus a relatively simple matter to enter appropriate formulae (cell addresses) to extract the numerical information from the TOTALS column of the cash-flow forecast into the account.

Two things you should note:

■ The Profit & Loss Account shows the performance of the firm over the year. Consequently, the total income generated by repairs is shown rather than the amount of money that has actually been received for carrying out repairs. Similarly, the total purchases made throughout the year are shown rather than the amount actually paid for.

■ In order to achieve these totals, the additional columns in the cash-flow forecast headed Adjustments must be implemented. It is this column that allows us to adjust the figures for credit payments and receipts.

We now need to enter the appropriate cell addresses and formulae to calculate the profit or loss of the firm. The contents are based on the cash-flow forecast as shown in Section 26 so, if you have used different cell locations to those shown in the illustration, you will need to adjust the cell locations used in the Profit & Loss account accordingly.

Projected Profit & Loss Account

```
┌─────────────────────────────────────────────────────────────────┐
│                                                                   │
│ Q1:                                                       READY    │
│                                                                   │
│                                                                   │
│         Q      R      S      T      U      V        W        X    │
│  1                        PROJECTED PROFIT & LOSS ACCOUNT          │
│  2                               1988                             │
│  3                                                                │
│  4                                    £             £             │
│  5              Revenue:                                          │
│  6              Repairs                     +N9+O9                │
│  7               Petrol                     +N10                  │
│  8                                          ---------             │
│  9              Total Revenue               +W6+W7                │
│ 10                                                                │
│ 11              Less Purchases              +N18+N19+O18+O19+P18+P19 │
│ 12                                          ---------             │
│ 13              GROSS PROFIT                 +W9-W11               │
│ 14                                                                │
│ 15                                                                │
│ 16              Less Expenditure                                  │
│ 17                                                                │
│ 18              Wages          +N20                               │
│ 19              Electricity    +N21                               │
│ 20              Rent           +N22                               │
│ 21              Rates          +N23                               │
│ 22              Telephone      +N24                               │
│ 23              Postage        +N25                               │
│ 24              Accountant     +N26                               │
│ 25              Sundries       +N27      @SUM(U18..U25)           │
│ 26                             -----     ---------               │
│ 27                                                                │
│ 28              NET PROFIT/LOSS             +W13-W25              │
│ 29                                          =========             │
│ 30                                                                │
│ 31                                                                │
│                                                                   │
└─────────────────────────────────────────────────────────────────┘
```

■ SECTION 28
Projected Profit & Loss Account

The Profit & Loss Account shown opposite is exactly the same as the one shown earlier, but the format of the numerical cells has been changed so that you can see the cell contents.

This is the Text format which is achieved by using the following sequence of commands:

Type **/**
Type **R**
Type **F**
Type **T** for Text
Highlight the range of cells required [**Enter**]

This allows you to see the actual contents of the cells in the range identified, i.e. formulae rather than their calculated results or labels with a label prefix rather than just the label.

Once entered, the Profit & Loss Account will automatically reflect any changes you make to the cash-flow forecast. Again, a window could be created so that the Profit & Loss Account could be on screen as well as the cell in which the changes are to be made.

Note If you make any structural changes to your cash-flow forecast, e.g. you add a new row for an expenditure that you have incurred but was not anticipated when you first entered the expenditure categories, don't forget to amend the Profit & Loss Account accordingly.

Break-even analysis

Break-even analysis is an important tool in short-term planning since it concentrates on the relationship between the four principal variables: cost, revenue, volume of output and profit.

Consider the following situation. Triform Ltd are considering the production of a product that they believe would sell for £10. Fixed costs of production have been estimated at £150,000 per year and variable costs are expected to be £4 per unit.

The problem facing Triform Ltd is how many units they would need to produce and sell before they start making a profit and consequently, what capacity should they make allowances for.

The worksheet opposite has been created to assist in the decision-making process.

Some explanation is required. The top half of the table is for user input. In this section, the variables can be changed to see the effect on the break-even quantity. For example, if Triform Ltd found a way of reducing fixed costs (purchasing a new, more efficient machine perhaps) to £120,000, then the break-even quantity would be immediately adjusted to 20,000. The other variables – fixed costs, total costs and profit – would also be adjusted accordingly. Having all this information available at the same time gives a very precise picture of how all the variables are affected by changes rather than just the break-even quantity.

The worksheet design

1   **The units row** was entered using the **Data Fill** command.   This allows consecutive cells to be filled with numbers and saves you typing each one individually. To achieve the result above:

> *Type* /
> *Type* **D** to select **Data**
> *Type* **F** to select **Fill**
> *Type* **B9..G9** (or highlight the fill range) [**Enter**]

You will be prompted for the **Start** number, the default being 0 [**Enter**]

You will be prompted for the **Step** number, the default being 1
> Type   1000 [**Enter**]

You will be prompted for the **Stop** number, the default being 8191.
> Type   50000 [**Enter**]

```
: A1: [W16] 'Selling Price                                    READY :
:                                                                   :
:        A           B        C        D        E        F       G  :
: 1  Selling Price      10                                          :
: 2                                                                 :
: 3  Fixed Costs     150000                                         :
: 4                                                                 :
: 5  Variable Costs       4                                         :
: 6                                                                 :
: 7  ----------------------------------------------------------------
: 8                                                                 :
: 9  Units               0    10000    20000    30000    40000   50000:
: 10                                                                :
: 11 Total Revenue       0   100000   200000   300000   400000  500000:
: 12                                                                :
: 13 Fixed Costs    150000   150000   150000   150000   150000  150000:
: 14 Variable Costs      0    40000    80000   120000   160000  200000:
: 15                                                                :
: 16 TOTAL COST     150000   190000   230000   270000   310000  350000:
: 17                                                                :
: 18 PROFIT        -150000   -90000   -30000    30000    90000  150000:
: 19                                                                :
: 20 BREAK-EVEN UNITS  25000                                        :
:                                                                   :
```

2   **Total revenue** is calculated by multiplying the selling price (B1) by
    the number of units (B9 to G9). To be able to enter the formula
    once and copy to the other cells, we must use *absolute
    addressing* as mentioned in Section 12. The relevant formula for
    cell B11 is $B$1*B9 (*note* 1-2-3 will automatically add a plus
    sign when you press Enter), which can then be copied to cells
    C11..G11.

3   **Fixed costs** are always the value that is entered in cell B3. We
    need to use *absolute addressing* once again so that we can copy
    the formula. This is achieved by typing $B$3 in B13 and copying
    to cells C13..G13.

4   **Variable costs** are calculated by multiplying the contents of B5 by the corresponding number of units in cells B9 to G9, so in B14 type $B$5*B9 and copy to cells C14..G14.

5   **Total costs** are a simple sum of Fixed and Variable costs, determined by typing +B12+B13 in B16 and copying to cells C16..G16.

6   **Profit** is calculated by subtracting **Total cost** from **Total revenue** − type +B11 −B16 in B18 and copying to cells C18..G18.

7   The **Break-even quantity** is calculated in B20. The formula is +B3/(B1 − B5), i.e. total fixed costs divided by the difference between the unit selling price and the variable cost per unit. Be sure to enclose the subtraction in brackets to 'force' 1-2-3 to perform this part of the calculation before the division.

Alternatively, or in addition to, you could set up an X-Y graph of the data as follows:

Select	**X range**	*Type*	**B9..G9 [Enter]**
Select	**A range**	*Type*	**B11..G11 [Enter]**
Select	**B range**	*Type*	**B16..G16 [Enter]**

The resultant graph will show two lines, one for **Revenue** and one for **Total costs**. It is the intersection of these two lines that provides you with the **Break-even quantity**.

Changing any of the values of the three variables in the input section of the model will obviously affect some combination of Revenue, Total cost and Profit, as well as the Break-even quantity. This will be shown immediately on screen due to the formulae used to create the model.

In addition, you can press F10 at any time in the READY mode to show a graph of the current data. This is particularly useful if you want to test 'What if?' situations and quickly view the effects on the break-even quantity in graph form.

Break-even analysis

With the initial data used for Triform Ltd your break-even chart should look like this after adding a title and the axes labels:

Break Even Chart

TRIFORM LTD

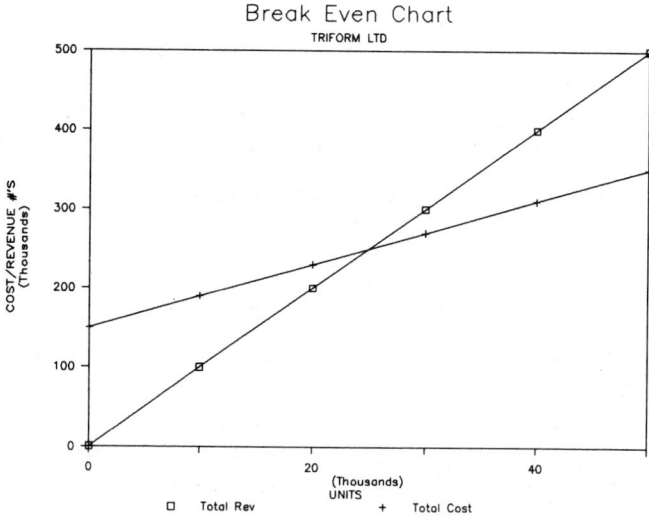

You can see from the chart that the break-even quantity given for the above circumstances is 25,000, which corresponds with the calculated number of units. From this information, Triform could establish the capacity required to meet the necessary output that would provide them with a suitable level of profit from producing their product.

A share portfolio

The model below shows a (short) list of fictitious shares, the current holding, price and value. You can make the list as long as you like (or can afford) — it will not affect the operation of the worksheet.

The model comprises two parts. To the left is the main body of the model which contains details of current holdings. To the right of this section, three adjustment columns are shown. These can be used to show the effect of buying and selling your shares. (You will notice the letters OK in this section; this will be explained in a moment.)

```
: A1: 'Share Portfolio                                              READY :
:                                                                         :
:                                                                         :
:        A       B        C        D       E    F     G        H          :
: 1   Share Portfolio                                                     :
: 2   ---------------                                                     :
: 3                                                  ADJUSTMENTS          :
: 4                                                                       :
: 5   Share   Current  Current  Current   :                     NEW       :
: 6   Name    Holding  Price    Value     :    BUY   SELL    HOLDING      :
: 7   ------------------------------------:    ------------------------   :
: 8   A          1000   3.97    3970.00   :                   3970.00     :
: 9   B          5000   2.50   12500.00   :                  12500.00     :
: 10  C          2000   2.87    5740.00   :                   5740.00     :
: 11  X          2000   1.23    2460.00   :                   2460.00     :
: 12  Y          5000   1.76    8800.00   :                   8800.00     :
: 13  Z          2000   1.95    3900.00   :                   3900.00     :
: 14  ------------------------------------:    ------------------------   :
: 15  TOTAL     17000   2.20   37370.00   :                  37370.00     :
: 16          ========         ==========                                 :
: 17                                                                      :
: 18                                                  OK                  :
: 19                                                                      :
: 20                                                                      :
:                                                                         :
```

■ SECTION 30
A share portfolio

The design

The formula in the Current Value column multiplies the contents of the Current Holding column by the contents of the Price column:

Type **+B8*C8** in cell D8, [**Enter**] and copy **To** D9..D13

The formulae in cells B15 and D15 give the total current holding and value by summing the contents of the relevant column:

Type **@SUM(B8..B13)** in cell B15, [**Enter**] and copy **To** D15

The value in cell C15 represents the average price of shares held and is found by dividing the total value by the total holding:

Type **+D15/B15** in cell C15 [**Enter**]

The New Holdings column in the adjustments section takes account of the current holding adjusted by the amounts entered in the Buy and Sell columns:

Type **(B8 + F8 − G8)*C8** in H8, [**Enter**] and copy **To** H9..H13

That is, the current holding of shares plus the number you intend to buy less the number you intend to sell, multiplied by the current price.

Whilst not obvious, cells D18 and H18 also contain formulae. They offer a means by which you can manage your portfolio and make use of the 1-2-3 **@IF** function. The general format is:

@IF(cond,x,y)

This says:
If the condition is *true* **then do x**
If the condition is *false* **then do y**

The functions in cells D18 and H18 check to see if the average share price is greater than £2 − this is the condition part of the @IF function. If it is, i.e. *true*, then nothing is displayed in cell D18 and OK is displayed in cell H18. If it is not, i.e. *false*, then D18 displays the message **SELL** and H18 displays the message **NOT ENOUGH**. The functions are:

@IF(C15>2," ","SELL")   in D18
@IF(H15/(B15 + F15 − G15)>2,"OK","NOT ENOUGH"   in H18

You will notice that F15 and G15 have been included in the second of the @IF functions and yet there appears to be nothing in those cells. In fact they contain formulae to sum the buy and sell columns, but their display has been suppressed. These totals are of little consequence to the model, but provide useful figures for the @IF function. The entries were made as follows:

Type **@SUM(F8..F13)** in F15, [**Enter**] and copy **To** G15
Type **/**
Type **R** to select **Range**
Type **F** to select **Format**
Type **H** to select **Hidden**
Type **F15..G15** (or highlight the range to format) [**Enter**]

Note If you require the results of the formulae in cells that have been 'Hidden' to be displayed in the future, simply reformat the cells to one of the other options available.

Operating the model

At its simplest level, the model can be used to test 'What if?' situations and the Adjustment section could be ignored altogether. Changing the current holding or current price will immediately show the effect the changes have on the total value of your portfolio.

The interesting part of the model, however, starts in the adjustments section.

Let's suppose that the price of 'B' shares falls to £1.50 (the market does fall occasionally!). If you enter this new price in cell C9 you are informed that the average price of your shares has fallen below £2 by the message SELL displayed in D18.

The adjustment columns are now used to test various combinations of buying and selling shares to restore the average price to more than £2. If an adjustment fails to do this, the message NOT ENOUGH will be displayed in cell H18.

One possible course of action is shown opposite.

When the average price reaches £2 due to the selling of 'B' shares, H18 displays the message OK. This, of course, substantially reduces the value of your portfolio and you may wish to test the consequences of buying other shares with monies received from the sale.

Once an action has been decided upon and implemented, the Current Holding column should be amended to take account of any transactions and the buy and sell columns cleared using the **/Range,Erase** command.

```
: A1: 'Share Portfolio                                        READY :
:
:
:         A       B        C        D       E   F    G         H      :
: 1   Share Portfolio                                                 :
: 2   ---------------                                                 :
: 3                                               ADJUSTMENTS         :
: 4                                                                   :
: 5   Share   Current  Current  Current  :                   NEW     :
: 6   Name    Holding  Price    Value    :  BUY  SELL     HOLDING     :
: 7   -------------------------------------  : -------------------------- :
: 8   A          1000   3.97   3970.00   :                 3970.00  :
: 9   B          5000   1.50   7500.00   :        3261     2608.50  :
: 10  C          2000   2.87   5740.00   :                 5740.00  :
: 11  X          2000   1.23   2460.00   :                 2460.00  :
: 12  Y          5000   1.76   8800.00   :                 8800.00  :
: 13  Z          2000   1.95   3900.00   :                 3900.00  :
: 14  -------------------------------------  : -------------------------- :
: 15  TOTAL     17000   1.90  32370.00   :                27478.50  :
: 16           ========        ===========                          :
: 17                                                                 :
: 18                          SELL                       OK          :
: 19                                                                 :
: 20                                                                 :
:                                                                    :
```

The @IF function should be changed to suit your own basis for managing the portfolio and to control the messages you want displayed. Just refer back to the general format before you enter the function to make sure it will give you the results you are looking for.

In addition to setting different criteria in the @IF function, the model could be developed by adding columns to show the commission payable on the buy and sell transactions you are 'testing'. This would give a more accurate guide to the number of shares you could buy with the available funds.

PART SIX

Administrative applications

■ SECTION 31
Introduction to administrative tasks

As 1-2-3 primarily manipulates numbers, it is often easy to forget the many other applications that it can be applied to. Administrative tasks are a good example. Speeding up the repetitive aspects of administrative procedures can save you time and money and bring a greater efficiency to your whole operation.

Some of the aspects have been covered already in earlier sections. If you require a cash-flow forecast, or any other worksheet, to be amended, your typist does not have to retype the whole document — simply amend the necessary data and reprint.

Some tasks, although possible with 1-2-3, are generally more efficiently completed with a word-processor. This would include addressing labels or envelopes ready for mailing.

There are other tasks which we will explore in the next few sections. All the applications covered here will have one thing in common — they require information to be shown in columns. As columns are an integral part of the spreadsheet package, 1-2-3 can be usefully employed in a variety of ways. At least you won't have to bother about setting tab stops every time you want to do column work!

Throughout the applications, there are really only two things considered:

■   The width of the columns.

■   The alignment of labels.

Manipulating one or both of these aspects allows you to create a neat and structured format for the particular item produced, clearly identifying categories of information and pertinent details. We will also make some use of the fact that long labels 'spill over' into the next cell, providing that cell is empty.

It is unlikely that you will arrive at a perfect format first time, every time so may I suggest the following procedure for each task you attempt:

1   Draft, on paper, a sketch plan of the outcome you would like to achieve with 1-2-3. This does not need to be exact as you will find that a general idea will be sufficient.

2   Use the default setting (9) for the column widths when you first begin the work in 1-2-3. These can be adjusted later when you have entered the data and can more accurately gauge the length of labels and text.

3   Use the default setting (left align) for the alignment of all text entries. Again, you will find it a more economical use of your time to align the labels to your requirements once the data has been entered.

4   Enter the data to approximate the sketch you have on paper. Rows and columns can be inserted or deleted later if the information is not quite 'spaced' to its best advantage.

5   Experiment with different printer settings to achieve the required result. Does the information have more visual impact when printed on A5 paper or do you need full A4 size?

Whatever you create, you can save it to disk and store it for use in the future. Any amendments can be quickly and easily made and reprinted as many times as you require with the minimum of time and effort.

With the applications that follow, the printed output is aimed at your customers. Do not miss the opportunity to impress them with the professional appearance of your price lists, invoices, menus, etc.

Creating and using price lists

A neat and attractive price list is an asset to any business from retail to restaurant. It is inevitable that the details on the list will need to be amended, probably several times as the business expands or introduces new lines and as prices fluctuate. You may also wish to mail your current price list to your customers with promotional literature, which means it will have to be reproduced several times. Creating the list with 1-2-3 makes all the above possible and easy to maintain.

The design

How your price list is designed will be determined by the information you require to be shown and the type of business it is designed for. However, most price lists are essentially columns of text and numbers which makes it an ideal application for 1-2-3 to handle. By organising the data with 1-2-3 you can quickly achieve the clarity of information that is required by your price list.

For example, take a cafe where several menus will be required and several aspects could change requiring the menu to be altered. Creating and storing menus with 1-2-3 could save you time and expense and enhance the appearance of the printed output.

A small menu is shown opposite as an example of what can be achieved with a little planning and design. I have excluded the column letters and row numbers so that you can see the output as the customer would see it. You could, of course, create the list anywhere in the worksheet.

There is nothing special about the entries made in the price list, but you can see the effect of having all the information neatly arranged in columns with the categories of fare clearly identified. The overall effect has been achieved by simply manipulating the column widths to suit the information. I used the following:

Column	Width	Column	Width	32/2
A	10	D	9	
B	7	E	9	
C	2	F	6	

```
  PRICE LIST
  ----------


     Beverages              Snacks
     ----------             ------
   Tea         0.30    Toasted Teacake   0.35
   Coffee      0.45    Cheese on Toast   0.50
   Chocolate   0.40    Pizza Slice       0.45
   Squash      0.25    Jacket Potato     0.40
   Milk        0.25
                       Sandwiches
   Cakes               ----------
   -----               Cheese            0.40
   Scone       0.25    Cheese & Onion    0.45
   Gateaux     0.60    Cheese & Relish   0.45
   Eclairs     0.40    Ham off the Bone  0.55
   Cheesecake  0.45    Chicken           0.50
                       Beef              0.65


  SERVICE AND VAT INCLUDED
```

You could also enhance the effect by printing the list on coloured paper bearing the company logo and/or instructing your dot-matrix printer to print in italics. (Simply change the wheel if you have a daisywheel printer.)

Once presented as an insert to a more substantial outer cover, the overall effect could be quite attractive.

For other types of businesses it may be important to give more information than is shown in the menu. This again could be achieved by adjusting the column widths to suit your data or by manipulating the alignment of headings. The price list below again shows how it would appear to customers.

Creating and using price lists

```
                    PRICE LIST
                    ----------

                                   Price per Box
         Order                     -------------
         Code    Description       1-3    3-5    5+

         -----------------------------------------------
         001     Unbranded ss/dd   6.50   6.25   5.99
         002     Unbranded dd/dd   8.50   8.25   7.99
         003     Unbranded dd/qd   9.50   9.25   8.99
         004     Datadisk ss/dd    7.95   7.75   7.50
         005     Datadisk dd/dd    9.25   9.00   8.75
         006     Datadisk dd/qd    11.75  11.50  11.25
         007     Truedisk ss/dd    7.90   7.70   7.40
         008     Truedisk dd/dd    9.00   8.80   8.50
         009     Truedisk dd/qd    11.25  10.95  10.70
         010     SafetySave ss/dd  8.15   7.95   7.75
         011     SafetySave dd/dd  9.15   8.95   8.75
         012     SafetySave dd/qd  11.15  10.95  10.75

         Inclusive of postage - just add VAT
```

With this price list I have left all the columns at the default width and let the long labels 'spill over' into the adjacent cells. Thus, the title 'Price List' is just stored in C1, 'Price per box' is stored in E3 and the note at the bottom in B20. All are left-aligned.

The headings for the prices columns are all right-aligned and the labels 'Order Code' and 'Description' are left-aligned.

You can see how the whole appearance of your price list can take on a completely different appearance simply by manipulating the column widths and/or the label alignment.

■ SECTION 33
Invoice preparation

All your credit customers will need to be invoiced for the goods they have received but not yet paid for. Using 1-2-3, you can speed up this operation, giving you or your staff more time to do other important tasks. In addition, the invoices can be sent to your customers promptly, thus helping to minimise the time taken by debtors to settle their accounts and improve your cash flow.

```
A1: [W5] 'J Trefer Ltd                                    READY


        A    B    C    D        E          F      G     H    I        J
  1  J Trefer Ltd                     To:
  2
  3                        INVOICE
  4                                       12-Jan-87
  5  --------------------------------------------------------------
  6                                           UNIT
  7  CODE   QTY    DESCRIPTION                 PRICE     AMOUNT
  8  --------------------------------------------------------------
  9  A1     20     SOCKS - Wool                1.95      39.00
 10  A5     10     SHIRTS                      8.95      89.50
 11  A8      5     BELTS - Leather             5.99      29.95
 12  A9      5     BELTS - Canvas              2.99      14.95
 13
 14
 15
 16
 17
 18
 19  --------------------------------------------------------------
 20                              AMOUNT TOTAL          173.40
 21
 22                                      VAT            26.01
 23
 24                              INVOICE TOTAL         199.41
 25                                              =========
```

The design

A completed invoice is shown on page 123.

The full model is created in two parts: the invoice itself and a corresponding price list.

The invoice format will depend upon your own particular needs and desires with respect to business address, headings and the column widths. The invoice above has been designed to be printed on standard A5 paper.

The second part of the model, the price list, is stored in a different part of the worksheet. This can effectively be anywhere in the worksheet, but in order to conserve disk space, it makes sense to have the two parts reasonably close together. I tend to store lists side by side rather than one on top of the other so that it is easy to add to the list at a later date if necessary. For this example, I stored the price list in columns K, L and M as shown below:

```
                                                    READY

        J       K       L       M       N       O       P       Q
    1           CODE    PRICE       DESCRIPTION
    2           ------------------------------
    3           A1          1.95 SOCKS - Wool
    4           A2         15.99 TROUSERS
    5           A3         39.99 JACKETS
    6           A4         11.95 SHIRTS - Lg Sl
    7           A5          8.95 SHIRTS
    8           A6         69.95 COATS
    9           A7         35.95 JKTS - Blouson
   10           A8          5.99 BELTS - Leather
   11           A9          2.99 BELTS - Canvas
   12           A10         2.95 TIE
   13
   14
```

■ SECTION 33
Invoice preparation

Entering the model

First, you will need to allocate codes to each of the products in your range. In this example, the product codes used are A1, A2, A3, etc. With a large range of products it can be difficult to remember which product has been allocated which code. You may wish to print a list of the codes with their corresponding product descriptions and keep this by the computer when the invoices are being prepared.

Next, design the invoice form. Experiment with widths of columns, headings, etc., aiming for an overall structure that 'looks right'. The invoice is going to your customers and creating a visually attractive and professionally produced form will create a good impression (though they may not necessarily pay you any quicker). For the above invoice, I set the following column widths:

Column	Width	Column	Width
A	5	F	3
B	3	G	10
C	5	H	3
D	3	I	9
E	20		

Columns G and I are formatted to two fixed decimal places.

Whilst not obvious, the columns headed 'Description', 'Unit Price' and 'Amount' on the invoice form, all contain formulae.

Description column

This information is extracted from the price list by the formula

   @VLOOKUP(A9,K\$3..M\$12,2)

This is the 1-2-3 **VLOOKUP** (vertical lookup) function which takes the following general format:

   @VLOOKUP(x,range,column number)

It operates by looking for the value x in the cells specified by **range**, moves the cursor to the right by the number of columns specified in **column number** and returns the contents to the cell in which the formula has been placed.

■ SECTION 33
Invoice preparation

Thus, the formula in the descriptions column will take the value placed in cell A9 (the code number), search for that number in the price list stored in cells K3 to M12 and move two columns to the right. The product description it finds corresponding to the code number will then be placed in the description column.

Unit Price column

The formula in the Unit Price column is again the @VLOOKUP function as used above, but the parameters are now

@VLOOKUP(A9,K\$3..M\$12,1)

Once the code number is entered in cell A9, the unit price corresponding to the product code will be placed in the Unit Price column.

Amount column

This contains a straightforward formula to multiply Quantity by Unit Price and is thus of the form **+C9*G9**.

Amount Total is simply the sum of the amount column and cell I20 contains the formula @SUM(I9..I18).

VAT   If the products you sell are VAT-rated then the amount can easily be calculated by 1-2-3. In the example above, it is assumed that all the products are liable to VAT at the standard rate of 15% and the formula in cell I22 is +I20*0.15.

Invoice Total is simply the Amount Total plus VAT and is calculated by the formula +I20+I22.

Depending on the version of 1-2-3 you are using, when you first enter the formulae either 0 (zero) or ERR will be displayed. Once you enter the Product Code and the Quantity this will change to reveal the result of the formula. However, this means that we cannot enter the formulae in all the possible rows of the invoice template without it becoming unsightly, unless all your invoices contain exactly the same amount of entries each time. This is the reason for the mixed addressing used in the @VLOOKUP functions so that we can copy them to those rows in which we make an entry. We will find a way around this problem in Part 9, when we look at macros, and offer a solution in Section 44.

■ SECTION 33
Invoice preparation

Dating the invoice

You will notice the date shown in cell G4. This, of course, could be typed in as you prepare the invoice, but 1-2-3 has a function that will do the typing for you – @**NOW**:

Place the cursor in G4
Type   @**NOW**[Enter]

The result will be a number. This is a serial number for the current date and time which, whilst interesting, is not much help to us on our invoices. However, we can format cell G4 so that the date makes sense:

Type   **/**
Type   **R**
Type   **F** to select **Format**
Type   **D** to select **Date**

You have several choices of Date format:

(DD-MMM-YY)   which will produce 14-Jan-88

(DD-MMM)   which will produce 14-Jan

(MMM-YY)   which will produce Jan-88

(Long Intn'l)   which will produce 01/14/88

(Short Intn'l)   which will produce 01/14

Note   Both the Long and Short International formats can be reconfigured using the command —
/Worksheet,Global,Default,Other,International,Date,
and then selecting the required format and pressing Enter:

Type   **1, 2, 3, 4** or **5**
You will be prompted for the **Range**
Type   **G4** [Enter]

The date displayed in cell G4 should now be in an acceptable format and will be automatically set to the date you entered when loading DOS (or as supplied by the internal clock), each time you retrieve the invoice file.

Now enter the price list. I have placed the price list to the right of the invoice, rather than below it, to avoid any problems with the changed column widths. The descriptions used should be comprehensible to

■ SECTION 33
Invoice preparation

both you and your customers and you will need to take account of their length when designing the invoice form.

Finally, we want to arrange the worksheet so that we can have a new (blank) invoice form on screen for each customer being invoiced. This can be achieved by storing the two parts of the worksheet in separate files on the disk. To ensure that the column widths and general layout are maintained throughout the operation you *must* follow this exact procedure which uses a new 1-2-3 command, **File Xtract**:

1   Press the **Home** key to place the cursor in A1.

2   *Type*   **/**
     Type   **F** to select **File**
     Type   **X** to select **Xtract**

3   You will be prompted for a file name:
     Type   **Invoice** [**Enter**]

4   You will be asked if you want to save the formulae in the worksheet as **Formulae** or as **Values**:
     Type   **F** to select **Formula**

5   You will be prompted for the **Xtract range**:
     Type   **A1..I25** (or highlight the range) [**Enter**]
     The file will be saved to disk.

6   Use the **Range** command to erase the contents of cells A1..I25.

7   Set the printer settings for the invoice. They will then be loaded into 1-2-3 with the price list so that you will only need to establish them once rather than every time you want to print the invoice. In this example, to print on A5 paper, I have used:

     Range: A1..I25
     Left margin: 5
     Right margin: 55
     Page length: 50

     Check this to ensure it works with your printer set-up.

8   Save the worksheet on screen as PLIST using the normal save command.

Operating the model

First, clear the screen so that you can fully see how the model operates:

Type /
Type **W** to select **Worksheet**
Type **E** to select **Erase**
Type **Y** to select **Yes**

Now retrieve the file you named PLIST.

We are going to load the invoice form on to the top of the PLIST file, enter the appropriate details, print the invoice and replace it with a blank form ready for the next customer's details. This makes use of the 1-2-3 command **File Combine**.

1   Make sure the cursor is in cell A1.

2   *Type* /
     Type **F** to select **File**
     Type **C** to select **Combine**
     You will be offered the choice of **Copy**, **Add** or **Subtract**.

3   *Type* **C** to select **Copy** (Do not select Add or Subtract)
     Type **E** to select **Entire File**
     Highlight **INVOICE.WK1 [Enter]**

4   Enter the Code number in A9 and the quantity in C9. Note the correct results are now displayed in place of 0 or ERR.

     Enter the code and quantity of the next item in A10 and C10, respectively. You now need to copy **From** D9..I9 **To** D10. This places the required formulae into the appropriate cells of the row you are operating in.

     Repeat this process until all the necessary entries have been made for this invoice.

5   Set up your printer, print the invoice (including a copy for your files) remembering that the print settings have already been established.

6   Repeat the **Combine** sequence to load a blank invoice form into the worksheet ready for the next set of customer details.

■ SECTION 34
Memo composition

Although 1-2-3 is not a word processor, basic paragraphs of text such as a memo can, with a little thought, be easily produced. This can be useful when you have a worksheet on screen that needs to be sent to a colleague with a note of explanation or instructions.

Design

There are several basic rules you should remember when producing a memo or other piece of text:

■ Memos take advantage of the fact that 1-2-3 can store up to 240 characters in a cell regardless of the column width.

■ All the lines of text you enter must be in the same column.

■ The text is entered as a series of long labels. It does not matter how much or how little information you enter in each label (except that no label can be greater than 240 characters in length).

■ The range containing your text can then be justified to produce a neatly formatted paragraph.

Memo composition

Procedure

Place the cursor in a blank part of the worksheet. The example below is shown in column A and beginning at row 30.

```
         A       B       C       D       E       F       G       H
28
29
30  TO:     Jo-Ann Shore
31  FROM:   David Humpage
32
33  DATE:   14-Jan-88
34
35  Below is the projected Profit & Loss Account for 1988.
36  This shows us in a healthy position but I am a little concerned
37  about the level of purchases.
38  Can you investigate the order levels and corresponding
39  discounts available from our major suppliers?
40  If you can let me have the details before the next board meeting
41  I will produce several projections
42  based on the discounts we could expect.
43
44
45
```

The 'labels' of text are typed to any length and consequently need to be justified to smarten up the appearance:

Type /
Type **R**
Type **J** to select **Justify**

You will then be prompted to enter the justify range. Two considerations have to be taken into account before you enter the range:

1 If there is nothing below the memo you only need to specify the range corresponding to the width you want the memo to be.

2 If, for example, you wanted to place the memo above the

Projected Profit & Loss Account, you can 'force' 1-2-3 to put the memo only in the space you have allocated and not allow it to affect whatever is below. To do this you would specify a range by giving the cell addresses of the top left and bottom right of the area available for the memo.

For the memo shown below, I selected a justify range of A35 to G35:

Type   **A35..G35 [Enter]**

```
|                                                                         |
|        A         B         C         D         E         F         G       H |
| 28                                                                        |
| 29                                                                        |
| 30  TO:    Jo-Ann Shore                                                   |
| 31  FROM:  David Humpage                                                  |
| 32                                                                        |
| 33  DATE:  14-Jan-88                                                      |
| 34                                                                        |
| 35  Below is the projected Profit & Loss Account for 1988. This          |
| 36  shows us in a healthy position but i am a little concerned           |
| 37  about the level of purchases. Can you investigate the order          |
| 38  levels and corresponding discounts avaliable from our major          |
| 39  suppliers? If you can let me have the details before the next        |
| 40  board meeting i will produce several projections based on the        |
| 41  discounts we could expect.                                           |
| 42                                                                        |
| 43                                                                        |
| 44                                                                        |
| 45                                                                        |
|_____|
```

You should experiment with different widths by selecting a variety of justify ranges until you find the setting that suits you best.

■ SECTION 34
Memo composition

Editing the memo

The normal editing functions are available to you when editing memos. So for example, if you wished to add the phrase *as a matter of urgency* immediately after *investigate* in row 37, you would proceed as follows:

Place the cursor in cell A37
Press **F2** to put you in Edit mode
Move the cursor to the relevant position and type the required phrase
Press Enter
Rejustify the paragraph using the **Range,Justify** command.

■ SECTION 34
Memo composition

Inserting the memo

It is quite likely that you will want to insert the memo to correspond with the particular aspect of the worksheet the memo refers to. This can be done by inserting sufficient blank rows to take the memo and using the **Move** command to place the text in the space you have just made available.

1   First, insert sufficient blank rows above the data in your worksheet:
Place the cursor in the top row of your data
Type   /
Type   **W**
Type   **I** to select **Insert**
Type   **R** to select **Row**
Move the cursor downwards to select the number of rows to insert
Press Enter

2   Move the cursor to the first row of your memo.

3   Invoke the **Move** command:
Type   /
Type   **M** to select **Move**

Highlight the whole of the memo — as the data is only stored in one colum you only need to highlight one column even though the highlight does not cover all of the text as it is shown on screen

Press Enter
You will be prompted to enter the range to move to
Type the cell address at which you want the memo to start
Press Enter

Remember   If you change the memo or rejustify it, you will need to specify a justify range for the length as well as the width to avoid your data below being knocked out of alignment.

With the memo now in the desired position above your data you can print the memo and the data together by ensuring you include both in the print range.

PART SEVEN

Managing a database

■ SECTION 35
What is a database?

Any information that can be grouped into like categories can be set up as a 1-2-3 database. For example, you could create a personal telephone directory of the names, addresses and telephone numbers of your acquaintances or a similar directory for your customers or suppliers.

Field names

The categories into which you group the information are known as **Fields** and each category must be assigned a **Field name**. In the case above, the field names would be *Name*, *Address* and *Telephone number*.

Records

Each unique set of information stored under the field names is a **Record**. In the case above, a single record would be, for example:

   J Watts   29 Main Street   540076

Databases

A database is, essentially, a collection of **Records**. If you consider a simple card index, then:

■   The card box would be equivalent to the database.

■   An index card would be equivalent to a record.

■   The categories of information stored on each card would be equivalent to the fields.

In 1-2-3 the **columns** become **fields**, the labels at the top of each column become the **field names** and the **rows** become **records**.

■ SECTION 35

What is a database?

The main advantages of a computerised database over a card index are:

■ The speed with which you can sort and extract records.

■ The ease with which you can create new records.

■ The amount of information that can be stored in a very small space.

■ The ease with which records can be amended and still retain their overall appearance.

■ The ease with which the details can be reproduced for interested parties.

The larger the database, i.e. the more records that need to be kept, the more advantageous the computer becomes.

■ SECTION 36
Database planning and design

As we have already noted for other aspects of using 1-2-3, it is essential that the database is planned before entering the information into the computer.

The best advice is to write the possible design on paper first, enter half a dozen records or so on the computer and then check that you can retrieve the information you will require from the database. If it needs some adjustment, or a major rethink, it is better to know about it now when you have only entered six records than when you have input all the required information. Entering the records in the first instance is the most time-consuming part of the whole operation and you will not want to do it twice!

Customer/supplier records

Suppose you wanted a database of all your customers and/or your suppliers. This could perhaps contain information on the company name, contact name and their telephone number. It would look something like this:

```
: A1: [W18] 'CUSTOMER DATABASE                                    READY :
:                                                                        :
:                                                                        :
:           A              B             C          D         E         :
: 1   CUSTOMER DATABASE                                                  :
: 2   -----------------                                                  :
: 3                                                                      :
: 4                                                                      :
: 5   COMPANY NAME      CONTACT NAME    TELEPHONE                        :
: 6   The Leather Rack  Deborah Mountain (0529) 633144                   :
: 7   Loud Record Shop  Nick Pratt      (0522) 225599                    :
: 8   Malam Garages     Philip Malam    (0529) 256745                    :
: 9   Forcenine         Gavin Roper     (0529) 374652                    :
: 10  Thingies          Anne Dredge     (0205) 345189                    :
: 11  Soft Toys Ltd     Stella Davey    (0772) 992653                    :
: 12  Stells            Stella Greenfield (0635) 827499                  :
: 13  Bat & Balls       Diane Appleby   (0205) 263785                    :
: 14  Covers Design     Annette Hall    (0524) 887392                    :
: 15  Jessies           Susan McIntyre  (0772) 117326                    :
: 16  K's Models        Karen Newby     (0529) 583724                    :
: 17  Picture Gallery   Victor Essel    (0522) 738293                    :
: 18  Paperback Parade  Jane Cooper     (0734) 100251                    :
: 19                                                                     :
: 20                                                                     :
```

You could then use the information simply as a telephone directory. This will be explored, along with other possibilities, in the following Sections.

However, before you start to build yourself a database, you should be aware of one or two rules relating to the construction of a 1-2-3 database, to ensure the sorting and selecting procedures work correctly:

- The first row of the database is 'reserved' for the field names.

- The second row must contain the first record of information.

- Each row of the database must contain a record. There can be no blank rows in a 1-2-3 database.

- Depending on the information to be stored, you will need to adjust the column widths if all the details are to be visible.

Other than that, you would enter the data exactly as for any other application of 1-2-3.

Note The telephone numbers have been entered as labels by preceding the entry with an apostrophe. This is to avoid the problem that would arise by having a space between the code and telephone numbers if you attempted to enter them as a number. An alternative would be to place the code and the number in two separate columns and enter them both as straightforward numbers.

As it stands, and however useful the information is to you, so much more could be added to give you a wealth of information at your finger-tips.

To the customer database you could add the full postal address so that envelopes or labels could be printed from it, details of their average order so that you could offer them special discounts on any order above a certain amount or details of which product they were most interested in so that you could mail them promotional literature on related products.

Your supplier database could also include the full postal address to be used for addressing envelopes or labels. In addition, you could include details of products they offer, discounts available and terms of payment.

The database you build should reflect the information peculiar to your circumstances and particular requirements.

■ SECTION 37
Sorting the records

The customer list shown in Section 36 shows the information entered at random with no thought given to the order in which the records should appear. For some applications, the order of the records may well be irrelevant, but often you will want the information shown in a particular order. The Sort command will allow you to place the information in a particular order very quickly.

For example, let's sort the customer list so that the company names are in alphabetical order:

> *Type* /
> *Type* **D** to select **Data**
> *Type* **S** to select **Sort**

The sort menu will appear:

```
:                                                                    :
: A1:                                                          MENU  :
: Data-Range  Primary-Key  Secondary-Key  Reset  Go  Quit           :
: Specify records to be sorted                                      :
:      A      B      C      D      E      F      G      H           :
: 1                                                                 :
: 2                                                                 :
:                                                                    :
```

Data-Range

You must first tell 1-2-3 the range of data to be sorted. This will usually be the whole database, but you *must not* include your field names or else these will be sorted along with your data.

Primary-key

This defines the field on which you want 1-2-3 to perform the sort. You select the primary sort key by typing the cell address of any cell in the column which holds the data to be sorted. You will then be prompted to indicate the sort order by typing **A** for ascending or **D** for descending.

Secondary-key

The secondary-key is an optional selection, but is available for you to distinguish between any records where the information stored in the primary field occurs more than once. You could set up a second field on which to sort by using this option. This can also be in ascending or descending order and does not have to be the same as for the primary-key.

Reset allows Range, Primary and Secondary-key settings to be returned to default.

Go instructs 1-2-3 to perform the sort using the conditions you have set.

Quit takes you back to READY mode.

Let us sort the customer list by company name in alphabetical (ascending) order:

    Type   **R** to select **Range**
    Type   **A6..C18** [**Enter**]
    Type   ***P to select Primary-key***
    Type   **A1** (or any other cell address in column **A**) [**Enter**]
    Type   **A** to select **Ascending order** [**Enter**]
    Type   **G** to select **Go**

If you were not watching the screen too carefully you will have missed 1-2-3 actually performing the sort. In fact, if you had watched the screen very carefully you would not have seen very much since the sort is so fast, particularly with a small database such as we have got, that it is difficult to notice that 1-2-3 is actually doing anything. However, if you check your screen you should find that the records have indeed been sorted and should now appear as shown opposite.

The searching of the database and finding and extracting records is left to the next section.

■ SECTION 37
Sorting the records

```
┌─────────────────────────────────────────────────────────────────────┐
│ A1: [W18] 'CUSTOMER DATABASE                                  READY   │
│                                                                       │
│                                                                       │
│             A              B            C          D        E         │
│  1   CUSTOMER DATABASE                                                 │
│  2   ------------------                                                │
│  3                                                                     │
│  4                                                                     │
│  5   COMPANY NAME       CONTACT NAME     TELEPHONE                     │
│  6   Bat & Balls        Diane Appleby    (0205) 263785                 │
│  7   Covers Design      Annette Hall     (0524) 887392                 │
│  8   Forcenine          Gavin Roper      (0529) 374652                 │
│  9   Jessies            Susan McIntyre   (0772) 117326                 │
│ 10   K's Models         Karen Newby      (0529) 583724                 │
│ 11   Loud Record Shop   Nick Pratt       (0522) 225599                 │
│ 12   Malam Garages      Philip Malam     (0529) 256745                 │
│ 13   Mr Thingies        Anne Dredge      (0205) 345189                 │
│ 14   Paperback Parade   Jane Cooper      (0734) 100251                 │
│ 15   Picture Gallery    Victor Essei     (0522) 738293                 │
│ 16   Soft Toys Ltd      Stella Davey     (0772) 992653                 │
│ 17   Stells             Stella Greenfield (0635) 827499                │
│ 18   The Leather Rack   Deborah Mountain (0529) 633144                 │
│ 19                                                                     │
│ 20                                                                     │
└─────────────────────────────────────────────────────────────────────┘
```

■ SECTION 38
Searching the database

The power of the database lies in its ability to **find** and **extract** records according to criteria that you determine; 1-2-3 can do this very quickly and, of course, very accurately. There is no possibility of the 'wrong' record being selected by mistake.

Before we can make use of the find and extract capabilities of 1-2-3, we must first establish the **Input range**, the **Criterion range** and the **Output range**.

The Criterion and Output ranges must be set up in a blank area of the worksheet and we will need the field names to be included. So before we establish these ranges, first copy all the field names to:

F4 for the Criterion range, and
F12 for the Output range

I have used the blank area to the right of the database so that the ranges will not interfere with adding records should this be necessary in the future. The columns have been adjusted to correspond to those of the database to ensure that all the details will be visible when we extract records to the Output range.

■ SECTION 38
Searching the database

Setting the Input range

The Input range defines all the records you want included in the search operations. This will normally be the whole database and *must* include the field names:

Type /
Type **D** to select **Data**
Type **Q** to select **Query**
Type **I** to select **Input range**
Type **A5..C18** [**Enter**]

Setting the Criterion range

The Criterion range is a range of cells in which you establish the basis on which you want the records to be selected. We established the area of the worksheet this would be by copying the field names to F4:

Type **C** to select **Criterion range**
Type **F4..H5** [**Enter**]

The range selected includes the row of field names and a blank row in which we will shortly type our criteria. (Because the row beneath the field names is currently blank, 1-2-3 would select all records if we performed a find or extract command. 1-2-3 interprets blank cells to mean that any entry in that field is acceptable.)

Setting the Output range

This range establishes where 1-2-3 will place the data once it has been extracted from the database. The area was established by copying the field names to F12. The field names were copied in the same order as they appeared in the Input and Criterion ranges, but you can place the field names of the output range in any order. This may be useful if you want to print the fields in a particular order once they have been extracted from the database:

Type **O** to select **Output range**
Type **F12..H12** [**Enter**]

Warning Selecting a single row output range, as we have done above, will erase any data stored *anywhere* in the columns below F12, G12 and H12. If you have data stored in the same columns identified as the output range, you must select a multiple-row Output range, e.g. F12..H24, which will comfortably contain the likely number of selected records.

■ SECTION 38
Searching the database

Setting the Criteria

The most interesting and powerful feature of the database function is the criteria by which records can be selected. This enables you to **Find** particular records that need to be edited or deleted and to **Extract** records from the database for printing.

The format in which you enter the criteria will be determined by the type of field on which the search is to be performed: text or numeric.

Text fields

You can instruct 1-2-3 to search for a particular piece of text by entering it exactly as it is in the database. For example, if you wanted all records with the surname Townsend, you would enter Townsend immediately below the field name **Surname** in the criterion range.

By using the 'wildcard' characters, query (?) and asterisk (*), you can also search the database for text which is similar in nature. The query matches any *single* character, e.g. B???s would match Baths, Bolts and Bells, but not Bats or Balloons.

The asterisk matches *all* characters to the end of the text, e.g. B* would match Baths, Bolts, Bells and Bats, plus any other word beginning with B. (*Note:* characters can be either upper or lower case.)

Numeric fields

To search for an exact match of a number, simply enter the value immediately below the appropriate field name in the criterion range.

However, you will find it is often more useful to select all those records that contain a value which meets a condition, e.g. all those records that contain a value greater than a particular number. To do this, we must use the **logical operators**:

< sets the condition to **less than** the value entered
<= sets the condition to **less than or equal to** the value entered
> sets the condition to **greater than** the value entered
>= sets the condition to **greater than or equal to** the value entered
<> sets the condition to **not equal** to the value entered

When using the logical operators above, you must also always use the cell address of the first record of the appropriate field. A typical entry would thus be:

+D5>1000 or +E2< = 5000

Multiple criteria

It is possible to set up very complex criteria under which to search the records in your database. For example, you may want to select records that match Townsend *and* Female *and* is a householder. Entering more than one criterion in *the same row* of your criterion range instructs 1-2-3 to search only for those records that match *all* the criteria.

Alternatively, you may wish to select all those records that match London *or* Manchester or Glasgow. Entering more than one criteria in *different rows* of the criterion range instructs 1-2-3 to search for those records that match *any* of the criteria. You will need to make sure that all the rows in which criteria have been entered have been included in the Criterion range.

Entering the criteria

The criteria must be entered whilst in the READY mode so:

Type   Q to select **Quit** from the **Query** menu

Suppose that we wanted to undertake a small tele-marketing campaign, to be aimed at our existing customers in Boston who we think may be interested in a new product or service recently introduced. The Boston dialling code is (0529) and so we need to set the criteria to search the database for all those records containing this code in the Telephone field. Thus, in cell H5,

Type   '(0529)*

Remember the apostrophe as this is a label. Including the asterisk in the criteria instructs 1-2-3 to search for all records that contain a telephone dialling code of 0529, *irrespective* of the number that follows, i.e. we want the information on all our customers in the Boston locality.

■ SECTION 38
Searching the database

Using the Find command

So that it makes changing the criteria easier later on, ensure you have the Criterion and Output ranges on screen before we Find and Extract records:

Type /
Type **D** to select **Data**
Type **Q** to select **Query**
Type **F** to select **Find**

The cursor will be placed in the first field of the first record in the database that matches the criteria set. This should be **Forcenine Gavin Roper**.

Press the down cursor key once and the cursor will 'jump' to the next record that matches the criteria. Repeatedly pressing the down cursor key will successively select each record that matches the criteria. When there are no more records that match the criteria, 1-2-3 will beep at you. You can move back through the records by pressing the up cursor key and to each field by pressing the right and left cursor keys.

The **Find** command is useful when you want to edit or view a particular individual or group of records. To edit, simply place the cursor in the entry to be edited, press F2 to enter Edit mode and use the cursor and delete keys to amend the record.

When you have finished with the **Find** command, press Enter and you will be returned to the Query menu.

Extracting the records

Whilst in the Query menu, we will instruct 1-2-3 to extract all those records that match our criteria and place them in the Output range:

Type **E** to select **Extract**

Several records should have been placed in the Output range and if all has gone well you should have on screen:

```
: H5: [W15] '(0529)*                                      MENU :
: Input  Criterion  Output  Find  Extract  Unique  Delete  Reset  Quit :
: Copy all records that match criteria to Output range          :
:       E          F              G            H        I   :
: 1            CRITERION RANGE                              :
: 2            ------------------                           :
: 3                                                         :
: 4            COMPANY NAME    CONTACT NAME    TELEPHONE     :
: 5                                           (0529)*       :
: 6                                                         :
: 7                                                         :
: 8                                                         :
: 9            OUTPUT RANGE                                 :
: 10           ------------------                           :
: 11                                                        :
: 12           COMPANY NAME    CONTACT NAME    TELEPHONE     :
: 13           Forcenine       Gavin Roper     (0529) 374652 :
: 14           K's Models      Karen Newby      (0529) 583724 :
: 15           Malam Garages   Philip Malam    (0529) 256745 :
: 16           The Leather Rack Deborah Mountain (0529) 633144 :
: 17                                                        :
: 18                                                        :
: 19                                                        :
: 20                                                        :
:                                                           :
```

Only records that match the criteria, i.e. have the Boston telephone dialling code, should appear in the Output range. This list could now be printed or used directly from screen to undertake your tele-marketing campaign.

Searching the database

Changing the criteria

Changing the criteria is a relatively simple affair but it must be done from the READY mode:

Type **Q** to select **Quit**

Your criterion range should still be on screen but if it isn't move the cursor so that the whole of the criterion and output ranges are visible.

We will now change the criteria so that 1-2-3 only selects the record that contains the contact name **Karen Newby**:

1   Erase the criteria set in cell H5.

2   *Type*   **Karen Newby** in cell G5

3   Press **F7**, the Query key.

The output range should now only contain one entry, the record containing the contact name **Karen Newby**.

Function key **F7** has the effect of repeating the last command used by Data Query. In this case, the last operation we performed was Extract, so F7 has repeated that operation for us from the READY mode without the need to return to the menus. This is, of course, particularly helpful if you need to make one or two changes to the criteria to select individual records.

■ SECTION 39
Estate agency database

Consider the details held by a small estate agency on the properties they have available for sale. They would include the number of bedrooms, the address, the price, whether or not there is an integral garage, etc. Such details could be easily grouped into categories (fields) and held in a 1-2-3 database. By setting the appropriate criteria, a client's requirements could be quickly entered and suitable properties listed on screen or via the printer.

A typical design is shown below:

```
A1: [W18] 'ESTATE AGENT                                      READY


               A        B    C    D      E    F    G        H
   1  ESTATE AGENT
   2  ------------
   3
   4
   5  ADDRESS          BEDS     STATUS   PRICE    COMMENTS
   6  29 High Street     3      Semi Det 45950    Carpets included
   7  14 James Street    3      Terrace  29000    Central Heating
   8  67 Vine Street     3      Semi Det 42000    Carpets included
   9  1 The Close        4      Det      75000    Twin Garages
  10  13 The Knoll       4      Semi Det 52000    Spacious Gardens
  11  47 The Folly       2      Semi Det 59000    Non Estate
  12  106 Campbell Road  3      Semi Det 37500    Needs Modernisation
  13  "The Beck"         5      Det      86000    1.5-acre grounds
  14  21 Cliff Way       2      Terrace  31000    Well Maintained
  15  35 Cliff Way       3      Terrace  37500    Carpets included
  16  54 George Street   3      Semi Det 61000    Sought after area
  17  9 Charles Street   2      Terrace  32500    Central Heating
  18  "Rose Cottage"     2      Semi Det 59500    Secluded Garden
  19
  20
```

151

Estate agency database

For this database, I set the following column widths:

Column	Width	Column	Width
A	20	E	8
B	5	F	3
C	3	G	9
D	9		

This was to give a more pleasing appearance to the database (sections will be printed out later) and allowed all the data to be viewed on screen at once.

However, it is immediately obvious that many other variables could be included in the database and, particularly with the use of codes, e.g. FDG for full double glazing and PDG for part double glazing, the information would not become 'too wide' to print across the width of standard A4 paper. The comments column could be dispensed with altogether if these aspects could be coded into individual columns. The print-out could then provide a very useful mailing list or introductory details for new clients.

The Criterion range has been set to K5..Q6 and the Output range has been set to K14..Q14. You will need to copy the field names to these locations and adjust the columns to the same widths as the database so that all the details will be visible in the Output range.

Setting the criteria

It is extremely unlikely that a client would be interested in just one aspect of a property and therefore you will need to set multiple criteria.

Let's say a particular client is interested in all properties in the area that have three bedrooms and cost less than £60,000. This would be entered as follows:

In cell **L6**   3
In cell **O6**   + E6< = 60000

Note   In criteria based on a logical operator, the cell address of the first entry in the Price field must be included.

The first criteria says only those properties with exactly three bedrooms should be found, and the second that they can cost anything that is equal to or less than £60,000, i.e. a price range of £0 to £60,000 inclusive.

Operating the model

Enter the details and ranges as discussed in the previous section. Don't forget to change the column widths of both A to G and K to Q if you want all the information to be on screen at the same time.

Enter the criteria that will instruct 1-2-3 to select all three-bedroomed properties costing up to £60,000.

Note   Because we are using logical operators for the criteria in O6, you should find that when you enter the criteria and press Enter, the number 1 is displayed in the cell. A logical operator will return the value 1 if the statement is **true** and 0 if the statement is **false**. In our case, the number 1 indicates that the first record in our database is a property that is priced at less than £60,000.

Go to the **Data,Query** menu and select **Extract**. This has now 'set' the Query command and consequently we can Quit the menu to return to the ready mode and use F7 each time we alter the criteria according to a client's requirements. This will make the whole operation run smoothly, impress the clients and minimise the time taken to produce a suitable list of properties.

Having selected **Extract**, your screen should now appear like this:

```
: 06: [W8] +E6<=60000                                          MENU :
: Input Criterion Output Find Extract Unique Delete Reset Quit :
: Copy all records that match criteria to Output range             :
:          K          L     M     N     O     P     Q     R         :
: 1   Criterion Range                                              :
: 2   ---------------                                              :
: 3                                                                :
: 4                                                                :
: 5   ADDRESS             BEDS    STATUS    PRICE   COMMENTS        :
: 6                        3                 1                      :
: 7                                                                :
: 8                                                                :
: 9                                                                :
: 10  Output Range                                                 :
: 11  ------------                                                 :
: 12                                                               :
: 13                                                               :
: 14  ADDRESS             BEDS    STATUS    PRICE   COMMENTS        :
: 15  29 High Street        3     Semi Det  45950   Carpets included :
: 16  14 James Street       3     Terrace   29000   Central Heating  :
: 17  67 Vine Street        3     Semi Det  42000   Carpets included :
: 18  106 Campbell Road     3     Semi Det  37500   Needs Modernisation :
: 19  35 Cliff Way          3     Terrace   37500   Carpets included :
: 20                                                               :
:                                                                  :
```

A print-out of the relevant section of the worksheet could be made so that the client can browse through the details, perhaps eliminating some properties on the grounds, for example, they do not like its location.

The example above means that the print-out would always show all the details relevant to the properties selected and can consequently limit the number of fields you can accommodate on standard A4 paper. However, you may find that once the criteria have been established, only some of the fields need to be printed. For example,

the records above all show that the properties have three bedrooms —
that was one of the criteria we set — so you may find it unnecessary
to include this information on the print-out; 1-2-3 can accommodate
this.

Selecting fields for the Output range

Instead of copying all the field names to the Output range we could
just copy those fields that we require to be printed out. The
corresponding information will be extracted from the database and
entered in the appropriate column.

Let's say you would be perfectly happy (because your clients would
be happy) just to have the addresses, prices and comments of all the
properties your client is interested in. We could reset the output range
on the following lines:

Erase the field names from the Output range K14..Q14
Copy or retype *exactly* the field names as they appear in your
database:
ADDRESS in K14
PRICE in L14
COMMENTS in N14
Reset the Output range to K14..N14

If you now select **Extract** by pressing **F7**, your output range should
appear as shown overleaf.

SECTION 39
Estate agency database

```
06: [W8] +E6<=60000                                          MENU
Input  Criterion  Output  Find  Extract  Unique  Delete  Reset  Quit
Copy all records that match criteria to Output range
         J              K          L   M    N      O     P      Q
1                  Criterion Range
2                  ---------------
3
4
5                  ADDRESS            BEDS    STATUS    PRICE   COMMENTS
6                                      3                 1
7
8
9
10                 Output Range
11                 ------------
12
13
14                 ADDRESS           PRICE   COMMENTS
15                 29 High Street    45950   Carpets included
16                 14 James Street   29000   Central Heating
17                 67 Vine Street    42000   Carpets included
18                 106 Campbell Road 37500   Needs Modernisation
19                 35 Cliff Way      37500   Carpets included
20
```

The main advantage of this type of approach is that you could have many more fields of information on which you could set criteria, but would not exceed the limit of the width of your paper when you come to print out the details for your client.

Estate agency database

You may like to experiment with setting criteria so that you can deal efficiently with any requirements of your clients. For example, I am interested in properties with three OR four bedrooms, providing the price is still less than £60,000. The criterion range must be changed to K5..Q7 and the criteria would need to be entered like so:

```
: J1:                                                     READY :
:                                                               :
:        J          K        L    M    N      O    P    Q       :
: 1                Criterion Range                              :
: 2                ---------------                              :
: 3                                                             :
: 4                                                             :
: 5                ADDRESS         BEDS  STATUS  PRICE  COMMENTS :
: 6                                 3             1             :
: 7                                 4             1             :
: 8                                                             :
: 9                                                             :
```

The entry in cell L7 is **4** to equate exactly with four bedrooms and in cell O7 + **E6<= 60000**, the same as is in cell O6.

On pressing **F7**, one record would be added to the Output range, that of 13 The Knoll.

To streamline the operation still further, you can automate the printing procedure so that all you have to do is press one key to print out the details for your client. Automating the repetitive aspects of your worksheet is the topic of the next part.

PART EIGHT

Let 1-2-3 take the strain : macros

■ SECTION 40
The basic concepts

A **macro** records a sequence of characters, words or commands which can then be executed by a single keystroke. This is a very powerful feature of 1-2-3 which allows you to speed up the entry of a complicated series of commands, store often-used formulae and labels and in many respects 'automate' the operation of your worksheet.

Macro rules

Learning to write macros is a little like learning a programming language. There are certain rules you must follow if your macros are going to be successful and there are several functions and concepts you have not come across so far:

■ All macros must be entered as **labels**. Consequently, formulae and numbers must be preceded by an apostrophe.

■ Each line of a macro sequence can be up to a maximum of 240 characters in length.

■ Each macro must be **named** before it can be executed. The macro name must be preceded by a **backslash** and 1-2-3 recognises only the letters A to Z as macro names.

■ Macros can be entered in one or several cells. If more than one cell is used, the macro must be entered in **consecutive cells** in **one column**.

■ Macros are executed by holding down the **Alt key** and pressing the key whose letter corresponds with the name given to the macro.

■ A macro will be terminated when it encounters a blank cell in the column where the macro has been stored or when it encounters the macro command {**Quit**} (or when it encounters an error).

■ Macros are automatically stored with the worksheet when it is saved and can be executed whenever that worksheet file is retrieved. Consequently, you are advised to store a brief explanation and the macro name somewhere close to the macro itself.

■ SECTION 40
The basic concepts

Some new keys will be used in this and the following sections. Perhaps you would like to locate them on your keyboard before we start to create a macro:

Tilde   This key is identified by a wavy line (~) and is situated immediately to the left of the large Enter key on some keyboards. The hash character (#) is located on the same key so you will need to use the shift key to type a tilde.

Braces   These are curly brackets ({}), which are located immediately to the right of the letter P key. Again, the Shift key will need to be used.

Backslash   This produces the character \ and is located immediately to the right of the left-hand shift key. *Do not confuse* this with the forward slash key (/), which is used to access the 1-2-3 command menus.

If the keys are not located on your keyboard as suggested above, a little searching may be necessary to find them.

Suppose that in a particular worksheet the word TOTAL was frequently required. To avoid repeatedly typing TOTAL many times, you can store the word as a macro and enter it with one keystroke.

Design

You will find it essential with all but the simplest of macros, to physically perform the keystrokes necessary to achieve the result you are aiming for and write them down on a piece of paper. Take entering the label **TOTAL**, for instance. You would have to:

> Place the cursor in the required cell
> Turn caps lock on (or press the shift key)
> *Type* **TOTAL**
> Press Enter or move the cursor

All of this can be placed in a macro. As we do not yet know in which cells the label is required, we will leave that type of operation to a following section and concentrate on the others.

Procedure

Start with a blank worksheet by saving whatever you have on screen if it is required or by erasing the worksheet:

> Place the cursor in B2
> Turn caps lock on
> *Type* **TOTAL**
> *Type* ~ [**Enter**]

The entry should look like this:

```
 ┌                                                              ┐
 │ A1:                                                  READY   │
 │                                                              │
 │                                                              │
 │        A      B       C      D      E      F      G      H    │
 │ 1                                                            │
 │ 2    \t     TOTAL~   Prints Total anywhere in the worksheet  │
 │ 3                                                            │
 │ 4                                                            │
 │                                                              │
 └                                                              ┘
```

Notice that I have made two other entries: \t and a brief description of what the macro will do. These labels are not strictly part of the macro, but serve to remind you in the future of the name of the macro and its usage. When you enter \t in cell A2, precede the backslash with an apostrophe or you will fill the cell with the letter t.

If you remember, 1-2-3 only recognises the letters A to Z as macro names. I have chosen **t** since it reminds me of the word 'total'. You will need to name all your macros by following this procedure:

Type /
Type **R** to select **Range**
Type **N** to select **Name**
Type **C** to select **Create**

If there are any other macros named in the worksheet, they will be displayed in the control panel. You should have no names displayed at the moment.

Type \t [**Enter**]

You will be prompted for the macro range. This only needs to be the first cell of the column in which the macro is stored:

Type **B2** [**Enter**]

Operating the macro

First, move the cursor to anywhere in the worksheet. The macro is invoked by holding down the **Alt** key and typing **T**, upper or lower case, it makes no difference. The word TOTAL should instantly appear in the cell just as if you had typed it from the keyboard.

Move the cursor to another part of the worksheet and invoke the macro again. No matter where you place the cursor, the word TOTAL will be entered when you invoke the macro.

To edit a macro

If your macro does not work, check to see where you have gone wrong and amend the entry as necessary. Entries in a macro sequence are edited in exactly the same way as any other cell entry. Either retype the whole entry or press F2 to put you in edit mode and alter the necessary keystrokes.

You do not need to rename or reset the range of a macro that you have

■ SECTION 41
Creating a simple macro

edited. This also applies to any additions you make to the macro, providing the entry is made in a consecutive cell in the same column as the other entries.

Before we leave this section to look at more complicated macros, remember:

If you get into any difficulty the macro can always be terminated by holding down the Control key and pressing Break. If Error is flashed by the mode indicator, you should press Escape.

■ SECTION 42
Special macro keys

All of the operations that can be performed from the keyboard can be included in a macro sequence. However, 1-2-3 requires certain commands to be entered in a particular way.

The function keys

Any of the function keys can be included in a macro sequence by simply enclosing the function **name** in braces. For example:

{**Edit**} has the effect of pressing function key **F2**
{**Goto**} has the effect of pressing function key **F5**
{**Windows**} has the effect of pressing function key **F6**

Moving the cursor

All the ways of moving the cursor that are available from the keyboard are available to a macro. Again, this involves enclosing a word in braces:

{**Down**} moves the cursor **down** one cell
{**Up**} moves the cursor **up** one cell
{**Left**} moves the cursor **left** one cell
{**Right**} moves the cursor **right** one cell

Where the movement is to repeated *in the same direction*, a number can be included to indicate how many cells the cursor should travel. For example, to move the cursor five cells to the right, you would enter:

{**Right 5**}

Note The space must be included between the command and the number.

{**Bigleft**} moves the cursor **left one screen**
{**Bigright**} moves the cursor **right one screen**
{**Pgup**} moves the cursor **up one screen**
{**Pgdn**} moves the cursor **down one screen**
{**Home**} moves the cursor to **A1**

■ SECTION 42
Special macro keys

Other useful keys

{**Blank A4**} erases the contents of A4 (or any other specified cell address or range).

{**Beep**} causes 1-2-3 to beep at you.

{**Quit**} terminates the macro.

{**Windowsoff**} suppresses screen display.

{**Windowson**} restores normal updating of the screen.

{**Paneloff**} suppresses the panel display.

{**Panelon**} restores normal updating of the panel.

{**?**} temporarily halts the macro whilst an entry is made from the keyboard.

All the commands enclosed by braces can be typed in upper or lower case without affecting their operation.

Automating printing and saving

Two operations you will find you are always performing are those of printing and saving your work. With a little care they can be entered as a macro sequence, saved with your worksheet and invoked when required.

The printing macro

As an example, this macro could be added to the PLIST worksheet to automate the printing of invoices. You will remember that the print settings are already saved with the worksheet so all that is required of the macro is to access the **Print** menu, **Align** the paper and **Go.**

Enter the macro as shown below, though not necessarily in the same cells:

```
: P1: '\p                                              READY :
:                                                            :
:                                                            :
:           P       Q       R       S       T    U    V    W :
: 1   \p       /ppag   Prints the invoice                    :
: 2                                                          :
: 3                                                          :
: 4                                                          :
:                                                            :
```

Add q to the sequence in Q1 to return to READY mode or agq to print a second copy for your files.

Note To enter the forward slash sign in Q1, which accesses the command menus, you must precede it by an apostrophe.

Name the macro \p, enter the range as **Q1** and invoke the sequence by holding down the **Alt** key and pressing **P** whenever you require the invoice to be printed. **Make sure your printer is ready to print before you invoke the macro.**

You could have this sequence stored with the PLIST file so that on the completion of an invoice it could be printed by holding down the Alt key whilst pressing P. With a little thought and the use of a {**branch**} command (see Section 44), the invoice could be printed automatically when the @IF function detects that the space bar has been pressed.

Automating printing and saving

The save macro

There are two possible macros for saving your worksheet. The first records a sequence of keystrokes which results in the worksheet on screen replacing an existing file on disk.

The second creates a new file, waits for you to enter a file name from the keyboard and then saves the file to disk.

The macro below replaces an existing file and a note has been entered to this effect adjacent to the macro:

```
┌─────────────────────────────────────────────────────────────────┐
│ P1: '\s                                                  READY    │
│                                                                   │
│          P       Q       R       S      T      U      V           │
│ 1   \s         {home}/fs~r Updates current file                   │
│ 2                                                                 │
│ 3                                                                 │
│ 4                                                                 │
└─────────────────────────────────────────────────────────────────┘
```

Note the use of {**Home**} to take the cursor to A1 before executing the saving routine.

The second save macro is shown below:

```
┌─────────────────────────────────────────────────────────────────┐
│ P1: '\s                                                  READY    │
│                                                                   │
│          P       Q       R       S      T      U      V           │
│ 1   \s         {home}/fs  Requests file                           │
│ 2              {?}~       name for saving                         │
│ 3                                                                 │
│ 4                                                                 │
└─────────────────────────────────────────────────────────────────┘
```

■ SECTION 43
Automating printing and saving

This macro makes use of the {?} command which temporarily halts the macro whilst you enter the filename from the keyboard. However, there are two things to remember when you include {?} in a macro sequence:

■ After making the required entry from the keyboard, you *must* press Enter to instruct 1-2-3 to continue with the macro.

■ Consequently, if you also want 1-2-3 to execute an Enter, the {?} must be followed by a tilde.

Writing 1-2-3 macros may not come easily to you − it certainly didn't to me. The macros created so far have been relatively straightforward to show some of the basic skills required. However, there is no substitute for experience so, try writing a few simple macros of your own. They do not need to be complicated, nor ultimately particularly useful, but once you have successfully written one or two you should feel more confident of tackling something on a grander scale.

As promised earlier, the macro in the next section deals with the unsatisfactory manner in which we were forced to enter the invoice details in Section 33. Whilst offering a more useful application of macros, it is more complicated than the macros attempted so far.

Automating invoice preparation

We found that the invoice preparation in Section 33 was unsatisfactory since when we entered the @VLOOKUP function into our template, a result of 0.00 or ERR was returned until we entered the details of Code number and Quantity. This made the completed invoice rather unsightly. We can overcome this problem with a macro so that the functions are entered automatically and only when they are required.

The design

The macro should be stored with the PLIST worksheet, so retrieve it from disk and use F5 to Goto P1.

Enter the macro **exactly** as shown below:

```
P1: '\s                                                        READY


          P      Q         R        S        T      U       V      W
 1   \s        {home}{down 8}{?}
 2             {right 2}{?}
 3             {right 2}@VLOOKUP(A9,K$3..M$13,2)
 4             {right 2}@VLOOKUP(A9,K$3..M$13,1)
 5             {right 2}+c9*g9
 6             {down}{left 8}
 7             {branch \c}
 8
 9   \c        {?}~{IF @CELLPOINTER("contents")=" "}{home}{quit}
 10            {branch \n}
 11
 12  \n        {right 2}{?}~
 13            {right 2}{up}/c~{down}~{down}
 14            {right 2}{up}/c~{down}~{down}
 15            {right 2}{up}/c~{down}~{down}
 16            {down}{left 8}
 17            {branch \c}
 18
 19
```

■ SECTION 44
Automating invoice preparation

What we have, in fact, is three separate macros 'linked' together by {**branch**} commands. Consequently, each individual macro should be named as shown above and the ranges identified as Q1, Q9 and Q12, respectively.

Most of the entries should be quite straightforward to follow and you should have no trouble with them. The one to be particularly careful about is the entry in Q9. Make sure you have a space between the word **IF** and **@CELLPOINTER** and that there is a space between the quotation marks after the equals sign.

What the macro does

The first part of the macro, \s, takes you to the first cell in which an entry is required − A9, for a code number. Using the Home key just provides the macro with a reference point from which to move. You could just as easily use {**GOTO**} and enter the cell address but {**Home**} and {**down**} serve just as well.

The {**?**} then halts the macro until an entry is made from the keyboard and Enter is pressed. You are then moved to the next cell where an entry is required, the quantity, and the macro again waits for an entry to be made and Enter to be pressed.

The macro then enters the relevant formula for the first line of the invoice. These are the @VLOOKUP functions and multiplication formula as described in Section 33. The cursor is then taken to the next cell where an entry is required − A10. An entry should be made and Enter pressed.

At this stage \c takes over the operation, being invoked by the {**branch**} command. This command terminates the current sequence of instructions and continues the execution at the cell determined by \c. The {Branch} command can be viewed as a Goto statement because it instructs 1-2-3 to 'go to' a new cell location for the next instruction. In this case it is used to go to a sequence designed to check what has been entered.

If a **code number** is entered then you are passed to \n via another branch statement, {**branch** \n}. This takes the cursor to the quantity column for an entry to be made from the keyboard, and when Enter is pressed, the relevant formulae are copied from the row above to complete the line. You are then passed to \c again, via {**branch** \c}, to check if you wish to enter another code number.

Automating invoice preparation

If the **space-bar** is pressed and followed by Enter, you are taken to the Home position and the macro ends due to the {quit} command. It is assumed that you have no more entries to make on this invoice and that you are ready for printing. (See Section 43 if you want to include a macro that will automate the printing procedure for you.)

This all occurs due to the lines

```
{IF @CELLPOINTER"contents" = " "}{home}{quit}
{branch \n}
```

The statement we have written says: 'If the cell content of the cursor's current position (C10 on the first pass) is a space, i.e. the space-bar has been pressed, then move the cursor to the home position, quit the macro and return to ready mode'.

If the content of C10 is not a space, i.e. you have entered another code number, then the statement says: 'Continue with the macro by moving to the next cell down the column'. Here you are passed to **\n** so that the remaining entries in the row can be completed.

The **@CELLPOINTER** function has a general format of:

@CELLPOINTER(attribute)

and can be used to discover several aspects of the current cell. These include the current cell address, the width of the current column and, as we have seen, the current cell contents. Take particular note of how the function has been used in this macro since it can be very useful in many applications.

Once you have grasped exactly how **\c** performs, you can experiment with what you would like to happen. For example, when you have finished typing the entries for one invoice you may not want to press the space bar, but enter Q for quit or some other letter or number. Instead of taking the cursor to the Home position you may wish to go to the Invoice Total cell to check the value of the invoice or you may want to call up a printing macro to immediately print the invoice. It is through this statement that all these things, and more, are possible.

When you have completed entering the macro you should resave PLIST.

■ SECTION 44
Automating invoice preparation

Operating the model

Basically, the model operates in the same way as the model we developed in Section 33, but now the macro moves the cursor for you and copies the formulae when and if they are required.

1   Load **PLIST** (now also containing the macro) and **combine** INVOICE so that we are in the start position and ready to enter the details of the first invoice.

2   Hold down the Alt key and type S to invoke the macro.

3   *Type*   **Code number** [**Enter**]
    The cursor will be positioned in cell C9 for you.

4   *Type*   **A number for the quantity** [**Enter**]
    The macro will now enter the @VLOOKUP functions and the multiplication formula in the appropriate columns. The cursor will then be placed in cell C10 ready for you to make the next entry.

5   If you type a new code number the sequence above will be repeated until you have completed all the necessary entries.

6   When you do not wish to make any more entries, press the **space-bar** and press Enter. The macro will then stop and you will be returned to the READY mode.

7   You are now ready to print the invoice.

Automating invoice preparation

Speeding up the macro

Because 1-2-3 is now doing a lot of the work for you, you may find that things are moving along a little too slowly and you are having to wait before you can make the next entry.

There are several ways of speeding up the process, but you must take care with all of them.

Manual recalculation will stop 1-2-3 automatically recalculating the whole worksheet every time an entry is made. Before you quit the macro, you *must* instruct 1-2-3 to perform a **Calc** operation. This would be achieved by including {**Calc**} in the macro immediately before {**quit**}.

{**windowsoff**} instructs 1-2-3 to suppress the screen display.

{**windowson**} returns 1-2-3 to normal screen display.

{**paneloff**} suppresses the control panel display.

{**panelon**} returns 1-2-3 to normal control panel display.

A certain amount of care should be taken in using the macro statements which control the screen display, particularly by the operator of the invoice program. Because nothing appears to be happening when both the panel and screen displays are suppressed, it is very easy to think that something has gone wrong and press a key (or several keys) to check the computer. This could make a mess of your invoice and mean you will have to start again. Most frustrating!

Automating entries into the database

Consider the customer database you entered in Section 36. You wish to add a new record (details of a new customer). Hopefully, this task will be repeated many times as your business grows and the advertising begins to pay for itself, so it is worth planning for the future by building a macro to record the sequence. The macro developed here relies on the fact that 1-2-3 databases must be created as a continuous 'block' of data, i.e. there can be no blank records. Consequently, we can find the 'extremes' of the database by using the End key and appropriate cursor key.

Entering the macro

The full macro is shown below as being entered to the right of the Criterion and Output ranges of the Customer database.

J1: '\s					READY

	J	K	L	M	N O
1	\s	{goto}A5~{end}{down 2}			Takes the cursor to
2		{branch \e}			the first blank row
3					available
4					
5	\e	{?}{right}{?}{right}'{{?}			Entries made from
6		{down}{left 2}			keyboard in all
7		{menubranch \c}			fields
8					
9					
10	\c	Continue	Quit		Select to continue
11		Add another record	Finish session		or Quit
12		{branch \e}	{branch \r}		
13					
14					
15	\r	/dsd{end}{down}~g			Database resorted
16		{goto}E1~			and returns cursor
17		{quit}			to Criterion range
18					

Again, the individual macros should be named as indicated above and the ranges identified as K1, K5, K10..L10 and K15. Take particular note that the range for \c covers *two* columns and that the Quit sequence is entered in **column L**.

Once the macro has been entered, the file should be **re-saved** under the same file name.

What the macro does

The macro begins by finding the first available blank row in which to place the new record. This is achieved by taking the cursor to the the cell address of the first field name, finding the last record by using the End key and the down cursor key and then placing the cursor in the row below.

The query command {?} is then invoked to await input from the keyboard and Enter to be pressed. You will be taken to each field in turn until the record is completed. A new macro function is then introduced − {**menubranch**}.

The macro \c is invoked by the {**menubranch**} command in cell K7.

The menu you create must take the following general format:

1st Column	2nd Column	3rd Column
Option 1	Option 2	Option 3
Description	Description	Description
Sequence of	Sequence of	Sequence of
keystrokes	keystrokes	keystrokes

The menu can have a maximum of eight options but each cell containing an option *must* be included in the macro range. One way to view {menubranch} is that each option created is treated as another individual macro. Consequently, the sequence of keystrokes should be entered in the same column as the option it relates to and will be terminated when a blank cell or {quit} command is encountered.

The {menubranch} command halts the macro sequence and presents you with a series of options of how the macro should proceed. The menu created is in an identical format to 1-2-3's own menus, i.e. the options appear in the second line of the control panel, a brief explanation of each option is given on the line immediately below and

Automating entries into the database

you make your selection by typing the first letter of the option or highlighting the option and pressing Enter.

Care should be taken in writing menus and the following points should be borne in mind:

■ As a menu option can be selected by typing the first letter, no two options should begin with the same letter.

■ Descriptions should be short, but informative.

■ Most menus should include the option to Quit and return to some particular stage of the operation or back to the READY mode

Selecting **Continue** from the menu returns the sequence to \e {**branch** \e} so that a further record can be entered.

If you select **Quit** from the menu, the macro automatically re-sorts the database in **\r** before returning control of 1-2-3 back to you via the {**quit**} command.

The macro in operation

Retrieve the Customer database file which should now also contain the macro.

Note   The macro makes use of 1-2-3's ability to retain the sort settings you established when you first entered the database, i.e. the sort range is defined as A6..C18, the primary-key is column A and the field will be sorted in Ascending order.

Suppose we wish to enter the details of two new customers:

Capital Letters, contact Michelle Sellers on (0772) 887463
Aperitifs, contact Karen Murfet on (0772) 445567

From anywhere in the worksheet:

Hold down the **Alt** key and type **S**
Type   **Capital Letters** [**Enter**]
Type   **Michelle Sellers** [**Enter**]
Type   0772) 887463 [**Enter**]
Type   **C** to select **Continue** from the menu
Type   **Aperitifs** [**Enter**]
Type   **Karen Murfet** [**Enter**]
Type   0772) 445567 [**Enter**]
Type   **Q** to select **Quit** from the menu

Automating entries into the database

Note When entering the telephone numbers in the above, the apostrophe (to ensure the number is entered as a label) and the opening bracket are entered by the macro in K5.

You should now be returned to the READY mode. The cursor should be in cell E1 and your Criterion and Output ranges should be on screen ready for you to perform an Extract command (press F6) or amend the criteria.

If you care to check your 'new' database, it should now look like this:

```
A1: [W18] 'CUSTOMER DATABASE                              READY


          A               B               C          D       E
  1  CUSTOMER DATABASE
  2  -----------------
  3
  4
  5  COMPANY NAME     CONTACT NAME    TELEPHONE
  6  Aperitifs        Karen Murfet    (0772) 445567
  7  Bat & Balls      Diane Appleby   (0205) 263785
  8  Capital Letters  Michelle Sellers (0772) 887463
  9  Covers Design    Annette Hall    (0524) 887392
 10  Forcenine        Gavin Roper     (0529) 374652
 11  Jessies          Susan McIntyre  (0772) 117326
 12  K's Models       Karen Newby     (0529) 583724
 13  Loud Record Shop Nick Pratt      (0522) 225599
 14  Malam Garages    Philip Malam    (0529) 256745
 15  Mr Thingies      Anne Dredge     (0205) 345189
 16  Paperback Parade Jane Cooper     (0734) 100251
 17  Picture Gallery  Victor Essel    (0522) 738293
 18  Soft Toys Ltd    Stella Davey    (0772) 992653
 19  Stells           Stella Greenfield (0635) 827499
 20  The Leather Rack Deborah Mountain (0529) 633144
```

The details of the two new customers have been added to the database and the records have been sorted in alphabetical order on the COMPANY NAME field.

■ SECTION 46
Debugging and auto-execute macros

Only a few aspects of creating macros have been covered in Sections 40 – 45. A browse through the macro section of your Reference Manual will confirm there are many more functions that can be incorporated in a macro sequence.

The macro facility is a very powerful feature of 1-2-3, capable of automating many complex sequences of keystrokes. The planning of a macro to suit a particular application can take many hours of work, but you will be rewarded with a smooth running, error-free application that can be repeated time and time again, even by people who have little or no knowledge of 1-2-3.

Debugging a macro

It is, perhaps, inevitable that there will be times when the macro you have created just does not perform how you intended, particularly when the macro is complex and contains several {**branch**} commands. To help you track down the problem(s), 1-2-3 has a **Step** feature that allows you to single-step through the macro until you find the offending entry.

The **Step** feature is invoked by holding down the **Alt** key and pressing **F2**. A STEP indicator will appear at the bottom of the screen to remind you that you are in Step mode. If you now invoke your macro in the normal way, you can execute the macro one keystroke at a time by repeatedly pressing any key. In between each step of the macro the STEP indicator will change to flashing SST to remind you that the macro is in process.

When the STEP feature encounters a {?} command you must press Enter to continue with the single-step operation.

When the error is located, leave the macro sequence by executing Break and edit the entry in the normal way. You will still be in STEP mode after editing so you can either invoke your macro and single-step through the sequence again or leave the STEP feature and return to READY mode.

To **exit** the STEP feature, hold down the **Alt** key and press **F2**. The STEP indicator will disappear.

■ SECTION 46
Debugging and auto-execute macros

Auto-execute macros

These are 'special' macros that will execute automatically when you retrieve the file from disk. Auto-execute macros are entered in a similar way to other macros except in two respects:

1   The macro *must* be named \0. Let me confirm that is zero and not an upper case letter O.

2   You can only have one auto-execute macro per worksheet. You may find auto-execute macros useful when the worksheet is to be used by someone other than yourself, particularly if they are not too familiar with the operation of 1-2-3.

The possibilities for applying macros to individual applications are almost endless, but remember to plan the macro first on paper by manually going through the keystrokes necessary to achieve the results you are looking for. Debugging a long macro can be very time-consuming.

PART NINE

Command
and function
summary

■ SECTION 47
Command summary

The lists in the following sections are not exhaustive, but cover all the commands functions used throughout this book.

This section should be used when you know what it is you want to do with 1-2-3, but cannot remember how to do it. If you require an example of a command in use, you should use the index to find the appropriate page in the text.

All commands are executed from the command menus which are accessed by pressing the slash key (/). An option is selected by either typing the first letter of the option or, highlighting the option and pressing Enter.

Changing the appearance of the worksheet

Change the alignment of one or more labels	/Range, Label
Change the format of one or more numbers	/Range, Format
Change the default label alignment	/Worksheet,Global,Label-Prefix
Change the default format of numbers	/Worksheet,Global,Format
Change the width of ONE column	/Worksheet,Column,Set-Width
Change the default column width	/Worksheet,Global,Column
Suppress the display of cell contents	/Range,Format,Hidden
Justify a range of text	/Range,Justify

Erasing cell contents

Erase the contents of one or more cells	/Range,Erase
Erase the whole worksheet	/Worksheet,Erase
Delete a whole column	/Worksheet,Delete,Column
Delete a whole row	/Worksheet,Delete,Row

■ SECTION 47
Command summary

Making cell entries

Copy the contents of one or more cells	/Copy
Move the contents of one or more cells	/Move
Merge current worksheet with file from disk	/File,Combine
Insert blank column ready to accept data	/Worksheet,Insert,Column
Insert blank row ready to accept data	/Worksheet,Insert,Row

File commands

Save the current worksheet	/File,Save
Save the current worksheet with password	/File,Save,[space],P
Save part of the current worksheet	/File,Xtract
Retrieve a worksheet	/File,Retrieve
Merge current worksheet with file from disk	/File,Combine
List worksheet files on disk	/File,List,Worksheet
List graph files on disk	/File,List,Graph
List print files on disk	/File,List,Print
List all files on disk	/File,List,Other

Printing commands

Set range to print	/Print,Printer,Range
Set/change print settings	/Print,Printer,Options
Align paper to top of page	/Print,Printer,Align
Print the current worksheet	/Print,Printer,Go

Command summary

Creating graphs

Select type of graph to be created	/Graph,Type
Specify data ranges	/Graph,X A-F
Add titles to the graph	/Graph,Options,Title
Create a key for the graph	/Graph,Options,Legend
Label the X axis	/Graph,Options,Title,X-axis
Label the Y axis	/Graph,Options,Title,Y-axis
Name the graph for future use	/Graph,Name
Save the graph for printing	/Graph,Save
Display the current graph on screen	/Graph,View
Reset the graph settings	/Graph,Reset
Print the graph	*See* Printgraph Program

Managing a database

Specify range of data to be sorted	/Data,Sort,Data-range
Select field on which to perform sort	/Data,Sort,Primary-Key
Specify the order of the sort	/Data,Sort,Primary-key,A or D
Perform the sort	/Data,Sort,Go
Specify range of data to query	/Data,Query,Input
Specify criterion range	/Data,Query,Criterion
Specify range for extracted records	/Data,Query,Output
Find the selected records	/Data,Query,Find
Extract the selected records	/Data,Query,Extract
Return to READY mode from the Query menu	Quit

Command summary

Miscellaneous commands

Change the start-up directory	/Worksheet,Global,Default, Directory
Set recalculation to manual	/Worksheet,Global,Recalculation
Create a window	/Worksheet,Window
Lock the row and/or column titles	/Worksheet,Titles,B or H or V
Fill a range with consecutive numbers	/Data,Fill

■ SECTION 48
Macro command summary

All operations that can be performed from the keyboard can be performed by a macro. A macro executes down a column and will be terminated if it encounters a blank cell, the macro command "quit· or an error. It is advisable to manually perform the keystrokes before entering the macro, label the macro with its name and enter brief details of its operation adjacent to the macro sequence. Your macro will be saved with the worksheet and can be invoked anytime the worksheet is on screen.

Move the cursor to the right	{right}
Move the cursor to the left	{left}
Move the cursor down	{down}
Move the cursor up	{up}
Move the cursor to cell A1	{home}
Move the cursor one screenful to the right	{bigright}
Move the cursor one screenful to the left	{bigleft}
Move the cursor one screenful down	{pgdn}
Move the cursor one screenful up	{pgup}
Pause and await entry from the keyboard	{?}
Continue the macro at a new cell address	{branch \a-z}
Pause and await selection from a menu	{menubranch \a-z}
Invoke a function key operation	{(function key name)}
Erase the contents of a cell or range of cells	{blank (cell address)}
Make the computer beep	{beep}
Suppress rewriting of the screen	{windowsoff}
Return to normal rewriting of the screen	{windowson}
Suppress rewriting of control panel	{paneloff}
Return to normal rewriting of control panel	{panelon}
Instruct the macro to press Enter	Type a tilde

Macro command summary

Instruct the macro to access the command menus	Type apostrophe before /
Terminate the macro sequence	{quit}
Name a macro sequence	/Range,Name,Create,a-z
Execute a macro	Alt a-z
Debug a macro in single-step mode	Alt F2
Return to READY mode from Step mode	Alt F2
The macro auto-executes when the file is retrieved	Name the macro \0

■ SECTION 49
Function summary

The functions in 1-2-3 are preceded by an 'at' (@) character and perform specialised calculations determined by the arguments you assign to it.

The general format for functions is:

@function name(argument1,argument2,...)

Logical operators

The following table shows the operators in the order they will be performed by 1-2-3 unless you override the precedence by enclosing an operation in brackets (parentheses).

Operator	Operation
	Exponentation
*	Multiplication
/	Division
+	Addition
−	Subtraction
=	Equal to
<>	Not equal to
<	Less than
>	Greater than
<=	Less than or equal to
>=	Greater than or equal to

■ SECTION 49
Function summary

Functions, format and operation

@**SUM** adds the contents of the range specified
Format: @SUM(cell address or range name)

@**NOW** returns a serial number which can be formatted to a date format with /Range,Format,Date
Format: @NOW

@**IF** If condition is True then perform x. If condition is false, perform Y
Format: @IF(cond,x,y)

@**VLOOKUP** looks for the value x in the first column of the range and moves the cursor to the right the number of columns specified in column number.
Format: @LOOKUP(x,range,column number)

@**HLOOKUP** looks for the value x in the first row of the range and moves the cursor vertically the number of rows specified in row number.
Format: @HLOOKUP(x,range,row,number)

@**CELLPOINTER** returns information – the attribute – about the current cell.
Format: @CELLPOINTER(attribute)

Index

Index

Index